Economics
and
Foreign Policy

INTERNATIONAL RELATIONS INFORMATION GUIDE SERIES

Series Editor: Garold W. Thumm, Professor of Government and Chairman of the Department, Bates College, Lewiston, Maine

Also in this series:

ARMS CONTROL AND MILITARY POLICY—*Edited by Donald F. Bletz**

THE INTERNATIONAL RELATIONS OF EASTERN EUROPE—*Edited by Robin Remington**

THE EUROPEAN COMMUNITY—*Edited by J. Bryan Collester**

INTELLIGENCE, ESPIONAGE, COUNTERESPIONAGE, AND COVERT OPERATIONS—*Edited by Paul W. Blackstock and Frank Schaf, Jr.**

INTERNATIONAL AND REGIONAL POLITICS IN THE MIDDLE EAST AND NORTH AFRICA—*Edited by Ann Schulz*

INTERNATIONAL ORGANIZATIONS—*Edited by Alexine Atherton*

LATIN AMERICA—*Edited by John Finan**

THE MULTINATIONAL CORPORATION—*Edited by Helga Hernes*

POLITICAL DEVELOPMENT—*Edited by Arpad von Lazar and Bruce Magid**

SOUTH ASIA—*Edited by Richard J. Kozicki**

SOUTHEAST ASIA—*Edited by Richard Butwell**

THE STUDY OF INTERNATIONAL RELATIONS—*Edited by Robert L. Pfaltzgraff, J*

SUB-SAHARAN AFRICA—*Edited by W.A.E. Skurnik*

U.S.S.R.—*Edited by David Williams and Karen Williams**

U.S. INVOLVEMENT IN VIETNAM—*Edited by Allan W. Cameron*

*in preparation

The above series is part of the
GALE INFORMATION GUIDE LIBRARY

The Library consists of a number of separate series of guides covering major areas in the social sciences, humanities, and current affairs.

General Editor: Paul Wasserman, Professor and former Dean, School of Library and Information Services, University of Maryland

Managing Editor: Denise Allard Adzigian, Gale Research Company

Economics
and
Foreign Policy

A GUIDE TO INFORMATION SOURCES

Volume 7 in the International Relations Information Guide Series

Mark R. Amstutz

Assistant Professor of Political Science
Wheaton College
Wheaton, Illinois

Gale Research Company
Book Tower, Detroit, Michigan 48226

Library of Congress Cataloging in Publication Data

Amstutz, Mark R
    Economics and foreign policy.

    (International relations information guide series ; v. 7)
(Gale information guide library)
    Includes indexes.
    1. International economic relations--Bibliography. 2. Interna-
tional relations--Bibliography. I. Title.
Z7164.E17A48 [HF1411]   016.33891   74-11566
ISBN 0-8103-1321-9

VITA

Mark R. Amstutz is currently assistant professor of political science at Wheaton College, Wheaton, Illinois. He received his B.A. from Houghton College and his M.A. and Ph.D. from American University, where he specialized in international relations. Amstutz has also taught at Nyack College and the American University and in Wheaton College's International Study Program in The Hague. Academic honors awarded him include the NDEA Title IV Fellowship and a summer grant from the National Endowment for the Humanities.

Amstutz has served as an editor for the United States Information Agency. He is presently working on an introductory reader in international political economy.

CONTENTS

Contents

ABBREVIATIONS

AID	Agency for International Development
CACM	Central American Common Market
COMECON	Council of Mutual Economic Assistance (of Soviet bloc countries)
ECLA	United Nations Commission for Latin America
EEC	European Economic Community
EFTA	European Free Trade Association
GATT	General Agreement on Tariffs and Trade
GNP	Gross National Product
IBRD	International Bank for Reconstruction and Development
IDA	International Development Agency
IDB	Inter-American Development Bank
IMF	International Monetary Fund
LAFTA	Latin American Free Trade Association
LDC	Less developed country
MNC	Multinational corporation
NATO	North Atlantic Treaty Organization
OECD	Organization for Economic Cooperation and Development
OEEC	Organization for European Economic Cooperation
OPEC	Organization of Petroleum Exporting Countries
SDR	Special Drawing Right
UNCTAD	United Nations Conference on Trade and Development

INTRODUCTION

The purpose of this study is to examine the information sources on economics
and foreign policy. The two areas are closely interrelated because economic
interests are an important dimension of foreign policy and because economic
transactions are a significant aspect of the international system. Although
economic phenomena have generally been regarded as an important aspect of
both foreign policy and the world system, scholarly interest in this area has
only begun to develop fully in the recent postwar era. One of the reasons
for this is that political scientists, who have traditionally dominated the study
of foreign affairs, have been primarily concerned with the political dimensions
of foreign policy and, more particularly, with the role of power among states.
Their interest has thus focused almost exclusively on international politics.
Economists, on the other hand, have been primarily concerned with international
economic relations and have given limited attention to the role of politics in
the nature and process of international economics. The result of the separation
of international economics from international politics has been that a plethora
of studies has developed on the theory and practice of each field, while only
a limited literature has emerged on the systematic relationship of economics to
foreign policy.

In the past twenty years, however, the tradition of maintaining a distinct separation between international economics and international politics has begun to
change. This shift has come about largely because of important developments
in the international system—developments which have resulted in an increased
role of economics in the foreign policy-making process and in the international
system itself. In part because of these changes, a renewed interest has developed in the relationship of economics to international politics. Indeed, the
interest in the interdisciplinary study of economics and foreign affairs has grown
so dramatically in the 1960s and early 1970s that a general framework for a
new subfield of the social sciences has begun to emerge, an area that might
be referred to as international political economy.

An important characteristic of this emerging field is its application of systematic political-economic analysis to the international environment. While our
study will focus on the limited but growing literature in this field, an attempt
will also be made to include the more general literature that perhaps is not as

systematic and distinctive as the studies on international political economy but which relates directly to the theme of this bibliographic study. Before describing more specifically the nature of international political economy and the concerns of this study, however, it will be useful to sketch some of the major changes that have encouraged the development of greater interest in the political economy of international affairs.

THE GROWTH OF ECONOMICS IN THE INTERNATIONAL SYSTEM

There are two contemporary developments in the international system that help to account for the increased importance of economics in the foreign policy process. First, the international system has become increasingly more economically interdependent because of the growing network of direct and indirect economic relationships among states. These interdependencies involve not only the growth of formal policies and actions of governments but also the increasing international economic transactions of business organizations. Because of the growth of public sector interdependencies, national economic conditions such as inflation, recession, unemployment, and the governmental policies designed to control such conditions are no longer of domestic concern only but also of interest to foreign states which may be affected by such policies and conditions. Nations have thus tended to become more vulnerable to foreign economic conditions, while at the same time increasing their ability to influence the economies of other states.

The growth of private economic interdependencies has perhaps had even more important consequences on the nation-state. Brought about largely by international banks, multinational firms, and other international business concerns, these nongovernmental interdependencies are significant because they are more widespread yet less perceptible than the deliberate economic policies of states. As a result, governments have found it increasingly difficult to control the growing network of private transnational relationships. Indeed, some scholars have suggested that the network of private economic interdependencies has become so influential and pervasive that they have predicted the demise of the nation-state.

The second important development in the international system is the increasing awareness of the role of foreign policy in promoting national economic growth. Although efficient production is an essential ingredient of economic development, national wealth is not achieved solely by balancing domestic consumption with domestic production, but rather by establishing an effective program of economic development within the framework of the international economy. Since autarky is not an effective strategy for developing the national economy, states must attempt to maximize national economic objectives within the structure of the international economy and pursue foreign economic policies that support the state's economic interests.

Of course, that domestic economic development is related to international economics is not a new realization or finding but a major tenet of the economic theory of comparative advantage developed by David Ricardo and other British political economists of the nineteenth century. What is new, however, is the increasing awareness of the relationship of international politics to the development and maintenance of domestic and international economic structures and policies. The growing awareness that political and economic phenomena are related in the international system has, in turn, encouraged statesmen to develop a political economy that integrates more carefully international politics and international economics. Perhaps one of the most dramatic attempts to apply this approach in the 1970s has been the establishment of the oil cartel by the Middle East oil-producing states. Given the success of this policy, it may be anticipated that other groups of states will attempt to combine political and economic power in a similar way in the future.

ECONOMICS AND FOREIGN POLICY

Since this study deals with the relationship of economics to foreign policy, it will be helpful to outline some important ways in which the two areas relate. To begin with, states pursue economic objectives within the international system. Because economic welfare is one of the most important concerns of a nation, foreign policy is designed, at least in part, to promote favorable domestic economic conditions. This means that governments will design commercial policies, negotiate trade agreements, request bilateral or multilateral economic assistance, and help establish international economic regulations that will allow them to maximize national economic interests either directly through public channels or indirectly through the private business sector. Moreover, states will attempt to work cooperatively with other states in order to establish an international economic framework that will both protect and increase national economic welfare. Since states are concerned not only with increasing standards of living absolutely but also with increasing their relative positions of wealth, states will seek to improve their level of economic development at every opportunity. This is why states attempt to confront and negotiate with other states over such issues as trade, investment, international monetary adjustments, and foreign economic assistance.

Secondly, economics relates to the foreign policy-making process. Foreign policy is not developed or designed by politicians and diplomats in a vacuum, nor is it carried out, as some theorists have suggested, by statesmen whose sole concern is the maximization of political power. Rather, foreign policy flows out organically from the nature of a nation's society. This means that if a foreign policy is to be effective in the long run, it must relate to the nature of a country's society, including its culture, social characteristics, economic interests of major social and economic groups, political values, and ideological concerns. This is particularly the case in a democracy where domestic interest groups play an important, if not essential, role in the making of foreign economic and political policy. Domestic interest groups also play a role in authoritarian states, however, for even in such countries the development of foreign policy often relates in some degree to the concerns of the nation's people. The development of foreign policy, in short, is subject to various forces that are partly economic in nature.

Thirdly, economics relates to the implementation of foreign policy. If foreign policy is to be effective, it must promote a country's national interests by taking into account the relevant political and economic conditions of the international system. More particularly, statesmen must take into account the formal international economic order and the less formal international economic interdependencies--the transnational economic forces of business firms, regional economic organizations, regional integration, and international factor movements. Since the international economic system is a part of the total framework in which foreign policy is implemented, it sets limitations on what can and cannot be done in the international system. The economic dimensions of the international system can therefore limit as well as enlarge foreign policy objectives that states may pursue.

The economic policies of foreign states also play an important role in the implementation of foreign policy. Since foreign policies are designed partially to compete for scarce political and economic resources, the pursuit of similar objectives will result in competition and possibly international conflict. As states attempt to develop an effective foreign policy, they must therefore take into account the nature, purposes, and capabilities of the foreign policies of other states. Unrealistic foreign policies--foreign policies that fail to take into account the political and economic interests and abilities of other states --will be largely ineffective.

THE FIELD OF POLITICAL ECONOMY

Much of the important literature on international political economy has been published in recent decades. This recent growth is largely the result of the late emergence, or perhaps reemergence, of the field of political economy.

Originally, both economics and political science were part of the study of moral philosophy. The birth of economics is generally dated from 1776, when Adam Smith published AN INQUIRY INTO THE NATURE AND CAUSES OF THE WEALTH OF NATIONS, a study that provided the foundation for the British school of political economy which was to dominate the field of economic analysis in the nineteenth century. The focus of the classical British economists was on the development of efficient production and distribution with a view of developing domestic and international policies. In the twentieth century, however, the study of economics shifted away from issues of public policy toward the development of a rigorous, positivistic body of knowledge by applying the scientific method and tools of mathematical analysis. The result of this increasing theoretical focus has been that the concerns with political economy and public policy have received limited scholarly attention by contemporary economists. Whereas political economy has been the main concern of British political economists, the concern of the twentieth-century economists has been largely the development of a pure theory of economics along with testable empirical hypotheses.

In contrast to economics, political science is regarded as both a new and old field of study. Some argue that the discipline of politics had its beginning in antiquity with the systematic study of the city-state by Greek philosophers. Others, however, tend to view the development of a separate, distinct field of political science as a relatively modern occurrence, dating from the early part of the twentieth century. Prior to the 1930s, the study of government and politics was generally associated with history, law, and moral philosophy, while the more specialized field of international relations was concerned with diplomatic history and international law. As students of politics increasingly adopted a positivistic methodology, however, political science became related less to normative issues and matters of public policy and more to the empirical, descriptive, and scientific aspects of social science. The development of contemporary political science reached its "take-off" stage in the 1950s with the arrival of the behavioral revolution, a revolution whose objective was to make the study of politics more scientific through the development of a body of deductive theory and empirical generalizations which could be tested and verified. While the implications of this revolution are still being worked out in the field of politics, it is clear that the developments of the past thirty to forty years have brought about a more specialized and theoretically mature discipline.

Along with the rise of the more positivistic, theoretically oriented social sciences, however, has come a growing chasm between the disciplines. As both political science and economics have become more distinct and methodologically refined, the difficulties of interdisciplinary study have tended to grow, thus increasing the barriers to the development of the field of political economy. The professions themselves have not encouraged their followers to depart from their airtight compartments in either discipline. Success in economics or political science has meant, to a large degree, grappling with the theoretical and methodological issues of a pure social science. Fortunately, the separation of these two disciplines has never been complete, and today there is a renewed concern and interest in the remarriage of the fields.

The renewal of political economy has come in two forms, one methodological and the other substantive. The methodological political economy--or what some have called the "new political economy"--is the attempt to use tools of economic analysis to examine political phenomena. Some examples of contemporary studies that have attempted to apply this methodological approach are Anthony Downs's AN ECONOMIC THEORY OF DEMOCRACY, Warren Illchmann and Norman Uphoff's THE POLITICAL ECONOMY OF CHANGE, and Bruce Russett's ECONOMIC THEORIES OF INTERNATIONAL POLITICS. The older and more developed form of political economy is the substantive concern with the interrelationship of political and economic phenomena. Albert Hirschman, a leading student of political economy, has suggested that this field be referred to as political economics, or "politics-cum-economics," to differentiate it from the methodological school. [1]

---

1. Albert O. Hirschman, A BIAS FOR HOPE: ESSAYS ON DEVELOPMENT AND LATIN AMERICA (New Haven, Conn: Yale University Press, 1971), p. 7.

Introduction

The rebirth of substantive political economy in recent decades has been due largely to the development of significant international problems that have encouraged interdisciplinary research. Among these tensions have been the need for international monetary reform, the role of the MNC, tariff and nontariff trade barriers, economic aid, defense economics, and regional integration. The increasing influence of economics in the international system, however, has been itself a consequence of two broad shifts in the world system during the postwar era. The first of these has been the shift from a bipolar to a multipolar system; the second has been the change from a highly charged ideological system to a world characterized by increasing economic interdependence. Because both of these shifts occurred during the early 1960s, it is possible to divide the postwar years into two rather distinct periods: the earlier era of ideological confrontation and the more recent era of economic interdependence.

The chief characteristic of the earlier period of the cold war was the continuing confrontation between two world powers--the United States and the Soviet Union. During this period both superpowers possessed an overwhelming monopoly of nuclear power and thus the fate of the international system rested largely on the actions or inactions of these two states. Although the East-West tensions were primarily political and ideological, both the United States and the Soviet Union attempted to gain support among the developing states by offering economic assistance. The assumption underlying these efforts, particularly by the United States, was that the best way to strengthen political relations was to improve economic conditions in the economically backward states. Because of the important role that economic aid played in the 1950s and 1960s, a significant literature developed on the political economy of foreign assistance, a literature that is examined in chapter 6.

Beginning in the early 1960s, the international system began to change fundamentally as the two world powers lost their monopoly of nuclear power. What originally was a simple bipolar system in the 1950s gradually began to appear more like a multipolar system in the mid-1960s as Japan, the People's Republic of China, England, France, and West Germany began to play more important economic and political roles in the world. Particularly significant in this shift was the increasing role of the LDCs, a group of seventy to eighty countries with close to two-thirds of the world's population. As these states began to assert their common concerns and challenge the political influence of the rich industrial states, they also became a major force in the new modified multipolar system.

The most important development that has resulted from the shift to multipolarity, however, has not been the increased number of states possessing nuclear power, but rather the shift in the fundamental values in the international order--a shift that has decreased the significance of ideological and political conflicts and increased the role of economic tensions. If the East-West tensions were predominately political, the tensions between the developed, industrial states (the North) and the developing nations of Africa, Asia, and Latin America (the South) have been primarily economic, focusing largely on the international economic inequities and methods by which these might be decreased. As a result, developing countries have tended to be particularly concerned with such economic issues as trade, the MNC, imperialism, foreign investment, and economic assistance. Of course, the new North-South conflict has not completely supplanted the older East-West tensions but it has created a new set of problems and concerns. The new interests in international economic issues, however, have not been exclusively a North-South issue, for the developed states themselves have had to deal with an increasing level of international economic tension among themselves. To be sure, the tensions between developed states have not been of the same magnitude of those between the developed and the developing states, but they have nonetheless emphasized the increased importance of economic phenomena in the international system.

Finally, it is important to note that the world system itself has undergone changes that have fundamentally altered the framework in which foreign policies are implemented. One of the most important of these is the growth of nongovernmental economic transactions between states--transactions over which sovereign states themselves have limited control but which exert a strong influence not only on a state's foreign policies but also on its domestic conditions. Because of the increasing interrelatedness of the world's nations, states can influence the political and economic behavior of other nations with greater facility. Indeed, the growing effect of one nation's actions on another is often not the result of a deliberate attempt to influence another state but rather the unintended consequence of close interdependency. One of the important implications of this increased level of world interdependency is that sovereign states are probably less sovereign than they used to be insofar as they find it more difficult to control the impact of the nongovernmental transnational forces. And as the level of these interdependencies continues to increase, it may be anticipated that the development and implementation of foreign policy will likewise become an increasingly more difficult task.

THE NATURE OF WORLD INTERDEPENDENCIES

Kindleberger has developed a useful model (see diagram, next page) for graphically portraying the various levels of international interdependency. The model is particularly helpful because it includes both political and economic phenomena at the domestic and international levels. Within the model six different levels of relationships are possible, only three of which are of interest to us here. First, there is a relationship between domestic economics and international politics, a relationship in which domestic economic phenomena may influence international politics and vice versa. For example, the level of a state's economic development is an important determinant of national power; on the other hand, an international condition of war will significantly alter the domestic economy by shifting production from peacetime goods and services to the necessities for waging war.

A second type of relationship is that between domestic politics and international economics. As with the first relationship, causality may move in

Introduction

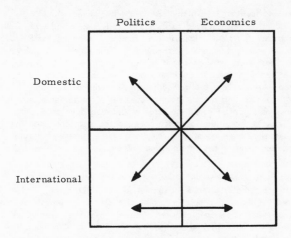

Reprinted, by permission, from Charles P. Kindleberger, POWER AND MONEY:
THE ECONOMICS OF INTERNATIONAL POLITICS AND THE POLITICS OF
INTERNATIONAL ECONOMICS (New York: Basic Books, 1970), p. 16.

either direction--from domestic politics to international economics and from the
latter to the former. When a government is forging its international economic
policies, such as those relating to trade, foreign investment, or international
monetary issues, domestic political interest groups will attempt to influence the
policy-making process in accordance with their own economic objectives.
Similarly, international economic phenomena such as the multinational corporations or regional common markets will themselves influence domestic economic
and political conditions in foreign states. Because of the increasing role of
the MNCs in the world, the poor, developing states have been particularly
concerned with the impact of these corporations on their nations' political
sovereignty.

A third level of interdependency is the relationship between international politics and international economics. Like the other levels of interdependency,
each of these variables may influence the other. An example of a condition
where international political phenomena influence international economic relations is the effect of detente on commercial relations between the United
States and the Soviet bloc. International economic change may itself influence
international politics, as has been the case in the European integration movement. The principal rationale for the establishment of the European Common
Market was to decrease the likelihood of war among Western European states
through an increase in economic integration.

Kindleberger's model, therefore, yields the following three interdependencies
of interest to this bibliography:

domestic politics ←————————→ international economics

domestic economics ←————————→ international politics

international politics ←————————→ international economics

THE NATURE OF THE LITERATURE

To assist the user of this guide, it will be helpful to make some observations about the studies included here. There is no well-defined body of systematic literature in international political economy. While the number of studies in this field has proliferated immensely in the postwar era, most of the literature still reflects a strong disciplinary bias toward either politics or economics. This is not surprising, since higher education has been primarily concerned with the training of economists and political scientists--not political economists. The increasing complexity of the world's international problems, however, has tended to force social scientists to adopt a more interdisciplinary perspective. The result of these pressures is that a small but growing number of economists and political scientists have begun to borrow concepts and theories from each other and combine professional efforts in order to more effectively analyze contemporary international issues. Since the development of international political economy has depended to a significant extent on these cooperative research efforts, future growth in the literature will depend greatly on continued professional cooperation.

Much of the literature is descriptive, in part because the major stimuli for publication in the field have been the tensions and problems that have developed within the international system. The literature on trade, international economic relations, integration, the international monetary system, and foreign aid, for example, is largely concerned with the presentation of data about particular political and economic problems, often followed by policy recommendations for dealing with the concerns that have been examined. The literature is thus informative of problems in international politics and international economic relations, but not highly analytical in quality.

The literature on imperialism and foreign investment, however, tends to be somewhat different, and there are at least two well-developed conceptual approaches evident in the studies in these areas. These two schools of international political economy might be called the orthodox and Marxist perspectives. The primary characteristic of the orthodox school is its assumption that the international economic and political order is intrinsically neutral--that is, the international environment is inherently neither good nor bad. Whether or not a state benefits economically or politically from the international system is determined not by the system itself but by the actions and policies of each particular state. Foreign investment and trade are not instruments for creating poverty and misery, as Marxists have often suggested, but tools that can serve both the developed and developing nations alike. Whether or not trade and foreign investment serve as engines of growth will be determined not by the environment but by the international economic relations established within the system. Studies on foreign investment from the orthodox point of view include

AMERICAN BUSINESS ABROAD by Charles Kindleberger, NATIONAL INTERESTS
AND THE MULTINATIONAL ENTERPRISE by Jack Behrman, SOVEREIGNTY AT
BAY by Raymond Vernon, and John Diebold's essay "Why Be Scared of Them?"

Another characteristic of the orthodox school of political economy is its belief
that imperialism is largely a political phenomenon. According to theorists of
this persuasion, imperialism--that is, the attempt by some states to dominate
others--is not caused solely or of necessity by economic motives or by international economic structures; rather, imperialism is largely the consequence of
an imperfect political system in which states find security by maximizing their
political power in the world. States seek political influence because it is the
only way that they can ensure that their interests will be protected. Studies
that represent this perspective include E.M. Winslow's THE PATTERN OF IM-
PERIALISM, P.T. Moon's IMPERIALISM AND WORLD POLITICS, Hans Morgenthau's POLITICS AMONG NATIONS, and Jacob Viner's essay "Finance and
Balance of Power Diplomacy." The most significant contemporary study of imperialism from the orthodox perspective is Benjamin Cohen's THE QUESTION
OF IMPERIALISM: THE POLITICAL ECONOMY OF DOMINANCE AND DE-
PENDENCE.

It is possible to subdivide the orthodox school of political economy, as Gilpin
has done,[2] into liberalism and mercantilism. Although both approaches assume
the relative neutrality of the international economy, they differ in two important ways. First of all, the liberal position assumes that international economic
relations are harmonious and that economic prosperity of all states can best be
maximized through increased international economic interdependence. Trade,
foreign investment, and a more integrated world economy will automatically
serve the economic interests of all states. Mercantilists, on the other hand,
assume that international economic relations are not necessarily harmonious and
that a nation's economic prosperity will not necessarily result from increased
international economic integration. States can best pursue their economic objectives not by allowing the automatic processes of international economic integration to dictate the economic policies of states, but by deliberately establishing policies that protect national economic interests from economic policies
and problems of other states. While the liberal position is primarily concerned
with internationalism, the mercantile view is principally concerned with
nationalism.

A second important difference between liberalism and mercantilism relates to
the relative importance of economics and politics in the international system.
According to liberalism, peace will automatically result from international economic harmony brought about by increasing economic integration and interdependence; in contrast, mercantilism assumes that the chief means to achieve
peace is through the manipulation of political power. Whereas liberalism

---

2. Robert Gilpin, U.S. POWER AND THE MULTINATIONAL CORPORATION:
THE POLITICAL ECONOMY OF FOREIGN DIRECT INVESTMENT (New York:
Basic Books, 1975), pp. 26-33.

assumes the primacy of economics over politics, mercantilism assumes the primacy of politics over economics. Studies such as Louis Baudin's FREE TRADE AND PEACE and Otto Mallery's ECONOMIC UNION AND DURABLE PEACE, which assume that trade and peace are positively related, and David Mitrany's A WORKING PEACE SYSTEM, which sets forth the theory that increased functional cooperation among states encourages peace, are representative of the liberal view of international political economy. Even a volume such as Raymond Vernon's SOVEREIGNTY AT BAY might be included in the liberal literature, for the underlying theme of that study is that increased world interdependence resulting from the MNC has been beneficial to the international system. Studies that represent the mercantile position include the essays "The Myth of National Interdependence" by Kenneth Waltz and "Obstinate or Obsolete? The Fate of the Nation State and the Case of Western Europe" by Stanley Hoffman, both of which question the view that the nation-state is becoming outmoded by the growth of economic interdependence in the contemporary international system.

The second major school of international political economy is Marxism. This school, along with the contemporary neo-Marxist perspectives which update and refine traditional Marxist theory, is characterized by the view that the international economic structures are not neutral but are the cause of interstate discrimination, exploitation, and uneven development. The problems of poverty, starvation, underdevelopment, and even war are not caused by insufficient natural resources, imperfect political systems, lack of incentives, or poor administration; rather, they are the consequence of an unjust and discriminatory international economic order. Since war and underdevelopment are a direct result of the system, Marxists believe that aggression, war, injustice, and poverty will be eliminated only when the imperialistic structures of capitalism are replaced. Aid, trade, and foreign investment will not alleviate the needs of the LDCs and, at worst, may even compound the problem of underdevelopment.

The Marxist position on the international political economy is perhaps best set forth in the theory of imperialism. The Marxist theory of imperialism was first developed in the early part of this century by such writers as Lenin, Nikolai Bukharin, and Rosa Luxemburg, but it has been refined more recently by such neo-Marxists as Andre Gunder Frank, Johan Galtung, Pierre Jalee, and Theotonio Dos Santos. According to the traditional theory, the principal reason why states seek to dominate others is to increase or preserve their national economic interests. Since the international capitalist system not only allows but encourages economic greed, powerful nations will attempt to increase their relative incomes by discriminating against the relatively poor, underdeveloped regions of the world. In the eyes of Marxists, colonialism was thus a logical outcome of the development of world capitalism.

The more recent expression of imperialism is the neo-Marxist theory of dependency, which has been set forth by Andre Gunder Frank in CAPITALISM AND UNDERDEVELOPMENT IN LATIN AMERICA and by Johan Galtung in "A Structural Theory of Imperialism." According to the theory of "dependencia," the world is divided into centers and peripheral areas, and any process of economic exchange between these two regions will distribute the gains from trade and production toward the capitalist centers within the LDCs and, more significantly, toward the major international centers--the rich industrial states of Western Europe and the United States.

The Marxist criticism of capitalist foreign investment, and in particular of the increased role of the MNC in the LDCs, is a logical extension of the general critique of the international political economy. Harry Magdoff, one of the leading North American Marxists, has argued in his study, THE AGE OF IMPERIALISM, that U.S. foreign policy has been designed primarily with the view of maximizing economic interests abroad, and the net result of U.S. overseas investment has contributed little to the development of the LDCs but has strengthened the military, political, and economic positions of the United States. The MNC has also come under attack from such neo-Marxists as Steve Hymer and Richard Wolfe, who argue that the international corporation is not an instrument for spreading economic development in the LDCs but of bringing increasing income inequality in the world. One of the most popular studies expressing this viewpoint is GLOBAL REACH: THE POWER OF THE MULTINATIONAL CORPORATIONS, by Richard Barnet and Ronald Mueller.

While the Marxist perspective has been presented most vigorously in the literature on imperialism and foreign investment, it has not been limited to these areas. There are many studies from the Marxist perspective on such themes as aid, trade, U.S. economic relations, and European integration. Teresa Hayter's AID AS IMPERIALISM and Michael Hudson and Dennis Goulet's THE MYTH OF AID, for example, critically analyze the aid programs of the United States and of selected international organizations from a neo-Marxist point of view. Their argument is essentially that aid is a palliative instrument which cannot serve to alter the fundamental social, political, and economic relationships that alone can bring development to the poor countries. Similarly, Johan Galtung's THE EUROPEAN COMMUNITY: A SUPERPOWER IN THE MAKING and Ernest Manel's DECLINE OF THE DOLLAR: A MARXIST VIEW OF THE MONETARY CRISIS present neo-Marxist critiques, respectively, of the European integration movement and of the international monetary tensions and reforms of the 1960s. Finally, American political institutions and foreign policy have been examined from the Marxist perspective by Richard Barnet in ROOTS OF WAR and by Michael Hudson in SUPER IMPERIALISM: THE ECONOMIC STRATEGY OF AMERICAN EMPIRE.

THE NATURE OF THIS STUDY

The purpose of this guide is to examine the most important information sources relating to economics and foreign policy. The editor has done this by compiling and annotating more than 750 books and articles in the field. Although every attempt has been made to annotate all bibliographical entries, some of the sources have not been annotated because of difficulties in locating materials.

It is important to emphasize that this study does not attempt to compile source materials that relate exclusively to either international politics or international economics. The literature in both fields is substantial and inclusion of either would have been far beyond the scope of this bibliography. This guide attempts, rather, to present the literature dealing primarily with political-economic interrelationships in the international system. Our concern is with the political economy of international relations, focusing both on the development and implementation of foreign policy and on the nature of the international system itself.

Chapter 1

INTERNATIONAL POLITICAL ECONOMY

International political economy is the field concerned with the interaction of political and economic phenomena in the international system. It is an emerging field characterized by a substantive concern with international issues, using the methods and tools of political economy. Since international politics and international economics are the foundations for this field, the first two parts of this chapter review briefly some of the basic literature in these areas. The third part deals with general theoretical studies on international political economy; part four examines the literature on transnational interdependencies.

A. INTERNATIONAL POLITICS

Hartmann, Frederick H. THE RELATIONS OF NATIONS. 4th ed. New York: Macmillan Co., 1973. xix, 715 p.

> Chapter 7 of this popular international relations text deals with economic issues relating to foreign policy, chiefly aid and trade.

Holsti, K.J. INTERNATIONAL POLITICS: A FRAMEWORK FOR ANALYSIS. 2d ed. Englewood Cliffs, N.J.: Prentice-Hall, 1972. 532 p.

> A popular college introduction to the field of international relations. Chapter 9 presents and evaluates various economic instruments of foreign policy by which a country may influence the behavior of another state. Special attention is given to foreign aid.

Morgenthau, Hans. POLITICS AMONG NATIONS: THE STRUGGLE FOR POWER AND PEACE. 5th ed. New York: Alfred A. Knopf, 1973. 618 p.

> One of the most influential international relations texts, based on a "realistic" interpretation of politics. Chapter 5 sets forth a political explanation of imperialism.

Palmer, Norman [D.], and Perkins, Howard. INTERNATIONAL RELATIONS; THE WORLD COMMUNITY IN TRANSITION. 3d ed. Boston: Houghton Mifflin Co., 1969. xxxv, 799 p.

> One of the most comprehensive international relations texts, with careful attention given to the relationship between international economics and international politics. See especially chapters 6, 7, and 19 on economic instruments of foreign policy, imperialism, and international economic relations, respectively.

Puchala, Donald J. INTERNATIONAL POLITICS TODAY. New York: Dodd, Mead & Co., 1972. xiv, 379 p.

> A general text that examines imperialism (chap. 5) and regional integration (chap. 6).

Rosecrance, Richard. INTERNATIONAL RELATIONS: PEACE OR WAR? New York: McGraw-Hill Book Co., 1973. xiii, 334 p.

> Attempts to use contemporary quantitative tools and behavioral approaches to present the field of international relations. Chapter 18, "Economic Statecraft," examines economic dimensions of peaceful and aggressive interstate behavior, including tariffs, quotas, depreciation, blockades, embargoes, and foreign assistance.

Rosenau, James N., ed. LINKAGE POLITICS; ESSAYS ON THE CONVER-GENCE OF NATIONAL AND INTERNATIONAL SYSTEMS. New York: Free Press, 1969. 352 p.

> A collection of pioneering theoretical essays on the interrelation-ship of domestic and international politics.

Singer, Marshall R. WEAK STATES IN A WORLD OF POWERS: THE DYNAMICS OF INTERNATIONAL RELATIONSHIPS. New York: Free Press, 1972. xii, 431 p.

> This international relations text focuses on the themes of power and interdependence. Chapter 6 deals with economic interdepen-dence.

Sprout, Harold, and Sprout, Margaret. TOWARD A POLITICS OF THE PLANET EARTH. New York: Van Nostrand Reinhold Co., 1971. 499 p.

> A general international politics text with limited attention given to economic phenomena.

Sterling, Richard W. MACROPOLITICS: INTERNATIONAL RELATIONS IN A GLOBAL SOCIETY. New York: Alfred A. Knopf, 1974. 648 p.

> Two chapters of this comprehensive text deal with international political economy. Chapter 8 discusses economic imperialism and the various theories connected with it; chapter 17 focuses on trade, the MNC, and the transnational movement of people.

B. INTERNATIONAL ECONOMICS

Ellsworth, Paul T., with the collaboration of Clark Leith. THE INTERNA-
TIONAL ECONOMY. 4th ed. New York: Macmillan Co., 1969. viii, 594 p.

> Chapter 6 of this popular introductory text examines selected con-
> temporary international economic issues, including monetary reform,
> economic integration, and trade liberalization.

Friedrich, Klaus. INTERNATIONAL ECONOMICS: CONCEPTS AND ISSUES.
New York: McGraw-Hill Book Co., 1974. 322 p.

> The following chapters of this well-balanced international economics
> text deal with policy issues: chapter 5 on economic integration,
> chapter 6 on commercial policy, chapter 7 on the MNC, chapter
> 13 on international economic policies, and chapters 14 and 15 on
> the international monetary system.

Kenen, Peter B., and Lubitz, Raymond. INTERNATIONAL ECONOMICS.
3d ed. Englewood Cliffs, N.J.: Prentice-Hall, 1971. viii, 127 p.

> A popular introductory international economics text focusing on
> the theory and practice of international trade.

Kindleberger, Charles P. INTERNATIONAL ECONOMICS. 5th ed. Homewood,
Ill.: Richard D. Irwin, 1973. xviii, 526 p.

> One of the most widely used international economics texts. The
> major subjects covered include trade theory, commercial policy,
> factor movements, and balance of payment adjustments.

Meier, Gerald M. THE INTERNATIONAL ECONOMICS OF DEVELOPMENT.
New York: Harper & Row, 1968. xi, 338 p.

> A theoretical analysis of various economic issues involved in the
> development process of the LDCs, including trade, aid, foreign
> investment, and international monetary reform.

Pearce, Ivor F. INTERNATIONAL TRADE. New York: W.W. Norton, 1970.
xxvii, 664 p.

> An upper-level text on international economic theory.

Pen, Jan. A PRIMER ON INTERNATIONAL TRADE. New York: Random
House, 1967. 146 p.

> A short, lucid, and nontechnical discussion of the objectives,
> process, and problems of international trade. A useful volume
> for the noneconomist.

Snider, Delbert A. INTRODUCTION TO INTERNATIONAL ECONOMICS. 4th ed. Homewood, III.: Richard D. Irwin, 1967. xvii, 476 p.

> This introductory text combines both theory and policy analysis. Part 1 is on trade theory, part 2 is on commercial policy, and part 3 is on international monetary relations.

Young, John P. THE INTERNATIONAL ECONOMY. 4th ed. New York: Ronald Press Co., 1963. xi, 795 p.

> This international economics text emphasizes problems and policy issues of the international economy.

C. INTERNATIONAL POLITICAL ECONOMY

Baran, Paul A. THE POLITICAL ECONOMY OF GROWTH. New York: Monthly Review Press, 1967. 308 p.

> A Marxist analysis of the process of economic growth.

Beer, Francis A. THE POLITICAL ECONOMY OF ALLIANCES: BENEFITS, COSTS AND INSTITUTIONS IN NATO. Beverly Hills, Calif.: Sage Publications, 1972. 37 p.

> The tools of economic analysis are used to examine the performance of NATO institutions.

Bergsten, C. Fred; Keohane, Robert O.; and Nye, Joseph S., Jr. "International Economics and International Politics: A Framework for Analysis." INTERNATIONAL ORGANIZATION 29 (Winter 1975): 3-36.

> Essay sketches some of the interrelationships between politics and economics in the international system.

Bergsten, C. Fred, and Krause, Lawrence B., eds. WORLD POLITICS AND INTERNATIONAL ECONOMICS. Washington, D.C.: Brookings Institution, 1975. xi, 359 p.

> One of the best collections of contemporary research in the field of international political economy. Originally published as Winter 1975 special issue of INTERNATIONAL ORGANIZATION.

Boulding, Kenneth E. CONFLICT AND DEFENSE, A GENERAL THEORY. New York: Harper & Row, 1962. 349 p.

> Boulding, a noted economist, uses the instruments of economic analysis to develop a rigorous framework for understanding conflict in the international system. The framework and instruments that are presented are useful in measuring the interrelationship of different variables. A sophisticated study.

Breton, Albert. "The Economics of Nationalism." JOURNAL OF POLITICAL ECONOMY 72 (August 1964): 376-86.

Using the tools of economic analysis, the writer develops a hypothesis of nationalism and draws policy implications using data from English-Canadian and French-Canadian nationalism.

Frohlich, Norman, and Oppenheimer, Joe A. "Entrepreneurial Politics and Foreign Policy." In THEORY AND POLICY IN INTERNATIONAL RELATIONS, edited by Raymond Tanter and Richard H. Ullman, pp. 151-78. Princeton, N.J.: Princeton University Press, 1972. 250 p.

The authors sketch an "entrepreneurial" theory of international politics based on assumptions about economic behavior.

Hirschman, Albert O. A BIAS FOR HOPE: ESSAYS ON DEVELOPMENT AND LATIN AMERICA. New Haven, Conn.: Yale University Press, 1971. 374 p.

A collection of essays on the political economy of development by one of the most distinguished contemporary political economists. Of particular interest is the introduction in which Hirschman examines the relationship between economics and politics. Previously published essays on foreign aid and foreign investment are also included.

_____, ed. LATIN AMERICAN ISSUES: ESSAYS AND COMMENTS. New York: Twentieth Century Fund, 1961. 201 p.

These essays analyze inflation, regionalism, land reform, and Latin American ideologies as they relate to the economic development of the region.

Illchman, Warren F., and Uphoff, Norman T. THE POLITICAL ECONOMY OF CHANGE. Berkeley and Los Angeles: University of California Press, 1969. xvi, 316 p.

Based on political science and economics concepts, a theoretical framework is developed to assist in the formulation of domestic public policy. The study makes an important contribution to the development of a "new" political economy.

_____, eds. THE POLITICAL ECONOMY OF DEVELOPMENT: THEORETICAL AND EMPIRICAL CONTRIBUTIONS. Berkeley and Los Angeles: University of California Press, 1972. xi, 506 p.

A collection of articles on the political economy of domestic political, economic, and social development.

Johnson, Harry G. " A Theoretical Model of Economic Nationalism in New and Developing States." POLITICAL SCIENCE QUARTERLY 80 (June 1965): 169-85.

Develops a theoretical model of economic nationalism in order to

explain the nationalistic economic policies of the LDCs. Policy
implications are developed from the model.

Keohane, Robert O., and Nye, Joseph S., Jr. "World Politics and the
International Economic System." In THE FUTURE OF THE INTERNATIONAL
ECONOMIC ORDER: AN AGENDA FOR RESEARCH, edited by C. Fred
Bergsten, pp. 115-80. Lexington, Mass.: D.C. Heath & Co., 1973.

Kindleberger, Charles P. POWER AND MONEY; THE ECONOMICS OF
INTERNATIONAL POLITICS AND THE POLITICS OF INTERNATIONAL ECO-
NOMICS. New York: Basic Books, 1970. vi, 246 p.

> A pioneering study on the relationship of international politics and
> international economics. The study examines two major themes--
> the economics of international politics (sovereignty, power,
> imperialism, war, and peacekeeping) and the politics of interna-
> tional economics (trade, aid, migration, capital movements, the
> international corporation, and the international monetary system).
> One of the most important contemporary studies on international
> political economy.

Knorr, Klaus. THE POWER OF NATIONS; THE POLITICAL ECONOMY OF
INTERNATIONAL RELATIONS. New York: Basic Books, 1975. x, 353 p.

> Knorr probes the complex interrelationships between power and
> wealth and attempts to show that the rich do not automatically
> become powerful in the international system and the powerful do
> not always carry out effective policies. Since much of the in-
> formation in the first seven chapters appeared in two of Knorr's
> earlier books--MILITARY POWER AND POTENTIAL and POWER
> AND WEALTH: THE POLITICAL ECONOMY OF INTERNATIONAL
> POWER (see chapter 9, section A, for both)--the most significant
> contribution of this study is the analysis of international interde-
> pendence in chapter 8 and imperialism and neocolonialism in
> chapter 9. This study is essential reading for anyone interested
> in the relationship between wealth and international power.

Mitchell, William C. "The New Political Economy." SOCIAL RESEARCH 35
(Spring 1968): 76-110.

> Reviews the methods, techniques, and problems of the "new"
> political economy--a field that seeks to apply the tools of eco-
> nomic analysis to the study of politics.

_____. "The Shape of Political Theory to Come: From Political Sociology
to Political Economy." In POLITICS AND THE SOCIAL SCIENCES, edited by
Seymour M. Lipset, pp. 101-36. New York: Oxford University Press, 1969.
328 p.

> Suggests new questions and methods appropriate for inquiry in the
> developing field of political economy.

Robbins, Lionel. MONEY, TRADE AND INTERNATIONAL RELATIONS. New York: St. Martin's Press, 1971. 282 p.

> This group of essays by the noted British political economist deals primarily with domestic and international economic concerns-- inflation, international finance, and trade policy. Chapter 10 is an excellent theoretical analysis of the economics of territorial sovereignty.

_____. POLITICS AND ECONOMICS; PAPERS IN POLITICAL ECONOMY. New York: St. Martin's Press, 1963. 230 p.

> A compilation of papers and addresses by Robbins on different themes of political economy. Although there are no essays on foreign policy, the materials present useful insights on the relationship between economics and politics.

Russett, Bruce, ed. ECONOMIC THEORIES OF INTERNATIONAL POLITICS. Chicago: Markham Publishing Co., 1968. 537 p.

> A collection of sophisticated methodological and theoretical essays on selected themes of economic analysis. The underlying assumption of the volume is that the rigorous tools of economics can be useful in developing greater understanding about the logic of international relations. Despite its title, no general economic theories that help to explain interstate relations are presented.

Strange, Susan. "International Economics and International Relations: A Case of Mutual Neglect." INTERNATIONAL AFFAIRS 46 (April 1970): 304-15.

> Strange bemoans the academic separation of politics and economics and suggests that the most important issues in foreign affairs can only be analyzed properly by using a combined perspective. Universities ought to develop rigorous programs in the political economy of international relations.

Wilber, Charles, ed. THE POLITICAL ECONOMY OF DEVELOPMENT AND UNDERDEVELOPMENT. New York: Random House, 1973. 434 p.

> Part 3 of this study on economic development in the LDCs examines contemporary perspectives on economic relations between rich and poor nations. Two essays examine the structure of international economic "dependence," while a third deals with the alleged imperialism of the World Bank.

D. WORLD INTERDEPENDENCY

Brown, Seyom. NEW FORCES IN WORLD POLITICS. Washington, D.C.: Brookings Institution, 1974. viii, 224 p.

> Brown argues that the cold war political alliances and the

traditional nation-state system are being challenged by the growth of social, technological, and economic transnational forces. This shift has been destabilizing because of the lack of effective international decision making. If the future world is to be a safe, orderly community, an increasing amount of coordination will be required. This study is one of the best accounts of the growing impact of transnationalism on world politics.

Camps, Miriam. THE MANAGEMENT OF INTERDEPENDENCE: A PRELIMINARY VIEW. New York: Council on Foreign Relations, 1974. 103 p.

This preliminary study examines some of the institutions, associations, and practices that will be required to manage the difficult problems resulting from increasing world interdependence. The study analyzes management problems in four areas--security, the international economy, development, and the conservation of natural resources.

Chadwick, Richard W., and Deutsch, Karl W. "International Trade and Economic Integration: Further Developments in Trade Matrix Analysis." COMPARATIVE POLITICAL STUDIES 6 (April 1973): 84-109.

This paper offers a sophisticated approach for measuring international transactions and then applies the methodology to the European integration movement.

Cooper, Richard N. "Economic Interdependence and Foreign Policy in the Seventies." WORLD POLITICS 24 (January 1972): 159-81.

Given the increasing economic interdependence of nation-states, governments must be prepared to face new types of political and economic pressures. Cooper suggests some possible effects of interdependencies on domestic and foreign policies of states.

_____. THE ECONOMICS OF INTERDEPENDENCE: ECONOMIC POLICY IN THE ATLANTIC COMMUNITY. Published for the Council on Foreign Relations. New York: McGraw-Hill Book Co., 1968. 283 p.

The central problem of this book is this: How can countries benefit most from economic cooperation while at the same time preserving the maximum degree of national autonomy? Cooper argues that economic interdependence of the nations of the Atlantic Community is increasing and that new balance of payments alternatives must be considered. Of three possible alternatives, Cooper believes that further integration can best be achieved by "deliberate imposition of barriers to the integrating forces, freedom of trade and international capital movements." Chapter 2 provides a short but useful summary of the postwar evolution of the international economic payments system.

_____. "An Economist's View of the Oceans." JOURNAL OF WORLD TRADE LAW 9 (July-August 1975): 357-77.

Examines some of the economically important ocean resources and proposes some principles by which their use can be regulated more effectively.

Deutsch, Karl W. "Nation and World." In CONTEMPORARY POLITICAL SCIENCE: TOWARD EMPIRICAL THEORY, edited by Ithiel de Sola Pool, pp. 204-30. New York: McGraw-Hill Book Co., 1967.

Attempts to explain the nature of nationalism and some of its major implications for maintaining peace and order in the world community. Although nation-states will continue to grow stronger and become more numerous, the problem of peace will become even more difficult. Deutsch offers suggestions as to how the force of nationalism might be moderated.

Deutsch, Karl W.; Bliss, Chester I.; and Eckstein, Alexander. "Population, Sovereignty and the Share of Foreign Trade." ECONOMIC DEVELOPMENT AND CULTURAL CHANGE 20 (July 1962): 353-66.

As countries increase in population and in their level of economic development, the level of trade as a proportion of the GNP will tend to fall. Population growth and economic prosperity tend to decrease the movement toward an integrated world economy.

Deutsch, Karl W., and Eckstein, Alexander. "National Industrialization and the Declining Share of the International Economic Sector, 1890-1959." WORLD POLITICS 13 (January 1961): 267-99.

Feld, Werner [J.]. NON-GOVERNMENTAL FORCES AND WORLD POLITICS; A STUDY OF BUSINESS, LABOR AND POLITICAL GROUPS. New York: Praeger Publishers, 1972. 275 p.

A pioneering empirical study of how the multinational corporation, international business groups, and transnational political parties affect the changing international political system. The author concludes on a cautionary note: while the nongovernmental forces of business, labor, and political parties do exert an important influence on the world political system, the real power lies with states, the chief authoritative political units in the world. An excellent source for transnational business and labor data.

Gardner, Richard H. "The Hard Road to World Order." FOREIGN AFFAIRS 52 (April 1974): 556-76.

Because of the impossibility of establishing world government in the short run, the most promising road to world order is through functional cooperation. "The hope for the foreseeable future lies not in building up a few ambitious central institutions of universal members and general jurisdiction as was envisaged at the end of World War II, but rather in the more decentralized, disorderly and pragmatic process of inventing or adapting institutions of limited jurisdiction and selected membership to deal with specific problems on a case-by-case basis, as the necessity for cooperation is perceived by the relevant nations."

Gilpin, Robert. "The Politics of Transnational Economic Relations." In TRANSNATIONAL RELATIONS AND WORLD POLITICS, edited by Robert O. Keohane and Joseph S. Nye, Jr., pp. 48-69. Cambridge, Mass.: Harvard University Press, 1971.

Gilpin argues that transnational economic relations are dependent on the politics of interstate relations. Far from eliminating the nation-state, transnational economic relations have been allowed to develop only when it was in the national interests of states to do so. The multinational corporation has been allowed to grow precisely because its development is in the national interest of the United States and other industrial states. The basic unit of international relations is and will continue to be the nation-state.

Helliwell, John. "Extractive Resources in the World Economy." INTERNATIONAL JOURNAL 24 (Autumn 1974): 591-609.

Rapid population growth, industrial development in the rich countries, and the uneven distribution of world stocks of extractive resources create tensions in the international system. Only by deliberate cooperation between the rich and poor states can a peaceful world order be forged.

Hollick, Ann L. "Seabeds Make Strange Politics." FOREIGN POLICY 9 (Winter 1972-73): 148-70.

A case study on how domestic interests--chiefly the oil and mineral firms, the fishing industry, the scientific community, and the U.S. Navy--influenced U.S. foreign policy toward seabeds.

Hollick, Ann L., and Osgood, Robert E. NEW ERA OF OCEAN POLITICS. Studies in International Affairs, no. 22. Washington Center of Foreign Policy Research, School of Advanced International Studies, Johns Hopkins University. Baltimore: Johns Hopkins University Press, 1974. vii, 131 p.

Hollick examines the basic political and economic issues regarding the use and control of oceans, while Osgood analyzes U.S. foreign policy interests in terms of the development of new international law principles governing the seas. The authors are directors of the U.S. Ocean Policy Project.

Howe, James W. INTERDEPENDENCE AND THE WORLD ECONOMY. New York: Foreign Policy Association, 1974. 63 p.

Juda, Lawrence. OCEAN SPACE RIGHTS; DEVELOPING U.S. POLICY. New York: Praeger Publishers, 1975. 318 p.

An analysis of the issues and problems relating to ocean space rights and of the developing international law in this area. Juda also examines U.S. foreign policy toward ocean rights and the domestic political forces that have helped shape it.

Keohane, Robert O., and Nye, Joseph S., Jr., eds. TRANSNATIONAL RELATIONS AND WORLD POLITICS. Cambridge, Mass.: Harvard University Press, 1972. 398 p.

One of the best collections of essays on different types of transnational relations. A number of essays on the economic dimensions of interstate relations are examined elsewhere in this study. Excellent bibliography.

Mendershausen, Horst. "Transactional Society vs. State Sovereignty." KYKLOS 22 (1969): 251-75.

The author views the increasing interdependence of the world and the breakdown of the bipolar international system as sources of instability and conflict. Increased international contact will not automatically bring peace.

Morse, Edward L. "Crisis Diplomacy, Interdependence and the Politics of International Economic Relations." In THEORY AND POLICY IN INTERNATIONAL RELATIONS, edited by Raymond Tanter and Richard H. Ullman, pp. 123-50. Princeton, N.J.: Princeton University Press, 1972.

The level of economic interdependence in the world has increased significantly in the postwar era, and this change has brought with it a number of developments, including the rise of economic crises. Diplomats and politicians have therefore been forced to wrestle with new, challenging international economic problems.

_____. "The Transformation of Foreign Policies: Modernization, Interdependence, and Externalization." WORLD POLITICS 22 (April 1970): 379-83.

An analysis of the consequences of modernization and world interdependence on foreign policy. Morse suggests that while these changes have increased domestic economic welfare, they have also increased the possibility of international instability.

_____. "Transnational Economic Processes." In TRANSNATIONAL RELATIONS AND WORLD POLITICS, edited by Robert O. Keohane and Joseph S. Nye, Jr., pp. 23-47. Cambridge, Mass.: Harvard University Press, 1971.

Contemporary international relations are much more interdependent than in previous decades because of the rise of transnational economic processes among states. Particularly important forces are population migration, capital mobility, and international trade. The critical issue in determining how transnational economic relations affect international politics is to assess the political importance of the changing levels of economic relations, and Morse offers some insights in dealing with this issue.

Nye, Joseph S., Jr. "Collective Economic Security." INTERNATIONAL AFFAIRS 50 (October 1974): 584-98.

A concise analysis of the beneficial and negative consequences of international economic interdependence. Nye suggests that international organizations can enhance the beneficial aspects of interdependence by providing data on trends in the world economy, regulating international economic practices, promoting international economic equity, and assisting in emergency situations.

_____. "Transnational Relations and Interstate Conflicts: An Empirical Analysis." INTERNATIONAL ORGANIZATION 28 (Autumn 1974): 941-96.

An empirical investigation of transnational Canadian-American relations during the postwar era. Nye found that while the importance of transnational relations organizations had increased during the period under examination, these changes did not strengthen the ability of the United States to achieve its objectives in bargaining with Canada. Canada's bargaining power, however, improved as a result of the shift in transnational processes.

Schmidt, Helmut. "The Struggle for World Product." FOREIGN AFFAIRS 52 (April 1974): 437-51.

Schmidt, the Minister of Finance of the Federal Republic of Germany, argues that if the world is to remain stable and peaceful, there will have to be closer cooperation among states. To do this, there must be "a fundamental change in patterns of behavior both among individuals and among nations." In the absence of world cooperation, the world will move toward disintegration, national isolation, and increased self-sufficiency.

Waltz, Kenneth N. "The Myth of National Interdependence." In THE INTERNATIONAL CORPORATION, edited by Charles P. Kindleberger, pp. 205-23. Cambridge, Mass.: M.I.T. Press, 1970.

Calling into question the common view that the nation-state is becoming an outmoded political entity, Waltz asserts that contemporary trade and foreign investment patterns have not and probably will not diminish the viability of the nation-state. Waltz writes: "The myth of interdependence both obscures the realities of international politics and asserts a false belief about the conditions that may promote peace."

Weiss, Mildred. "The Lawless Depths: The Need for an International Oceans Regime." In THE U.S. AND THE DEVELOPING WORLD: AGENDA FOR ACTION, 1974, edited by James W. Howe, pp. 95-106. New York: Praeger Publishers, 1974.

Discusses the need for managing ocean resources. Some of the major international tensions on ocean regulations are examined along with U.S. policies toward some of the issues.

Weiss, Thomas G., and Jordan, Robert S. INTERNATIONAL ADMINISTRATION AND GLOBAL PROBLEMS: AN ANALYSIS OF THE WORLD FOOD CONFERENCE. New York: Praeger Publishers, 1975. 150 p.

A case study of the 1974 World Food Conference held in Rome, focusing on preparation, deliberation, and follow-up.

Chapter 2
INTERNATIONAL ECONOMIC RELATIONS

This chapter examines the significant contemporary literature on the international economic order, the institutions facilitating and regulating transnational economic relations, and selected aspects of the bilateral economic relations of the United States and other countries. The literature on the international economy and economic relations is particularly large and therefore an attempt is made to include only those studies in which analysis is based on the interdisciplinary perspective of political economy. Since some of the issues pertaining to international economic relations are examined elsewhere in this study, it is advisable that other chapters be used in connection with this one. The themes which relate most closely to this chapter are trade (chapter 3), regional integration (chapter 4), and the international monetary system (chapter 5).

A. THE INTERNATIONAL ECONOMIC SYSTEM

Behrman, Jack N. TOWARD A NEW INTERNATIONAL ECONOMIC ORDER. Paris: Atlantic Institute for International Affairs, 1974. 80 p.

> International peace can only be achieved if there is international economic justice. Unfortunately, most attention is given to the development and refinement of rules for the allocation of economic goods, but little attention is ever given to the fundamental issue of whether the system itself is just and adequate. Behrman discusses a number of issues that must be examined if a more just international economic system is to be established.

Bergsten, C. Fred, ed. THE FUTURE OF THE INTERNATIONAL ECONOMIC ORDER: AN AGENDA FOR RESEARCH. Lexington, Mass.: Lexington Books, 1973. xv, 357 p.

> The most important essay in this anthology is R. Keohane and J. Nye's study (chap. 15) of some of the major political issues of the international economic system. Also useful is Bergsten's discussion (chap. 1) of some significant research issues in the field of international political economy.

Bhagwati, Jagdish N., ed. ECONOMICS AND WORLD ORDER: FROM THE 1970'S TO THE 1990'S. New York: Macmillan Co., 1972. 365 p.

A collection of essays by a group of noted economists on the world order conditions likely in the year 2000.

Cooper, Richard N., ed. A REORDERED WORLD; EMERGING INTERNATIONAL ECONOMIC PROBLEMS. Washington, D.C.: Potomac Associates, 1973. 260 p.

An excellent collection of articles on important contemporary international economic issues. The articles, all of which were published earlier in FOREIGN POLICY, focus on the international monetary system, economic relations with the LDCs, the allocation of world resources, and the relationship of economics to foreign policy.

Corbet, Hugh, and Jackson, Robert, eds. IN SEARCH OF A NEW WORLD ECONOMIC ORDER. New York: John Wiley & Sons, 1974. 288 p.

A collection of articles on different themes of the international economic system. See in particular the following: H. Corbet, "Commercial Diplomacy in an Era of Confrontation"; H. Malmgren, "The Need for a New System for World Trade and Payments"; and H.G. Johnson, "General Principles for World Monetary Reform."

DiMarco, Luis Eugenio, ed. INTERNATIONAL ECONOMICS AND DEVELOPMENT; ESSAYS IN HONOR OF RAUL PREBISCH. New York: Academic Press, 1972. xix, 515 p.

These essays, written in honor of the Argentine economist Raul Prebisch, examine theoretical and empirical issues of international economics. See in particular: Charles P. Kindleberger, "Direct Investment in Less-Developed Countries: Historical Wrongs and Present Values"; John P. Powelson, "The International Politics of Latin American Economics"; and Harry G. Johnson, "The Crisis of Aid and the Pearson Report."

Fleming, Harold M. STATES, CONTRACTS, AND PROGRESS; THE DYNAMICS OF INTERNATIONAL WEALTH. New York: Oceana Publications, 1960. 128 p.

Part 1 of this brief volume analyzes problem areas between sovereign states and foreign private businesses, including nationalization, property rights, and contractual obligations. Part 2 examines methods of transfering wealth between states.

Gilpin, Robert. "Three Models of the Future." INTERNATIONAL ORGANIZATION 29 (Winter 1975): 37-60.

A penetrating analysis of three contemporary models of international political economy: 1) the sovereignty-at-bay or liberal model, which views the state as becoming obsolete because of increasing economic interdependencies; 2) the dependencia or Marxist model, which views the nation-state system as a means of capitalist exploitation through imperialism; and 3) the mercantilist model, which views economic interdependency as coming to an end and being replaced by economic nationalism.

Hansen, Roger D. "The Politics of Scarcity." In THE U.S. AND THE DEVELOPING WORLD: AGENDA FOR ACTION, 1974, edited by James W. Howe, pp. 51-65. New York: Praeger Publishers, 1974.

A discussion of the increasing world commercial tensions of the 1970s and their possible impact on U.S. economic policies. Hansen believes there could be increasing economic tensions if states cannot agree upon new commercial policy guidelines. Offers policy suggestions.

Ingram, James C. INTERNATIONAL ECONOMIC PROBLEMS. 2d ed. New York: John Wiley & Sons, 1970. 182 p.

A discussion of important problems facing the international economic system, including tariffs, integration, international finance, and world monetary arrangements.

Jenkins, Robin. EXPLOITATION: THE WORLD POWER STRUCTURE AND THE INEQUALITY OF NATIONS. London: MacGibbon & Kee, 1970. 224 p.

Using political, economic, and sociological approaches, the author examines the interaction of states in the world community, focusing on relations among rich states, among rich and poor states, and among poor states.

Jensen, Finn B., and Walter, Ingo, eds. READINGS IN INTERNATIONAL ECONOMIC RELATIONS. New York: Ronald Press, 1966. 578 p.

A collection of policy-oriented articles focusing on trade relations, the international monetary system, aid, and foreign investment.

Meier, Gerald M. PROBLEMS OF COOPERATION FOR DEVELOPMENT. New York: Oxford University Press, 1974. xii, 249 p.

This study explores the ways governments, international organizations, and multinational corporations can help devise policies and programs that will aid the economic development of the LDCs. Three issues are examined: aid, investment, and trade.

Myrdal, Gunnar. ECONOMIC THEORY AND UNDERDEVELOPED REGIONS. New York: Harper & Row, 1957. 168 p.

Based on the theory of circular and cumulative causation, Myrdal explains why regional inequalities have persisted within and between nations. The only way to deal with this problem is to introduce planning in the LDCs.

_____. AN INTERNATIONAL ECONOMY: PROBLEMS AND PROSPECTS. New York: Harper & Row, 1956. 381 p.

The eminent Swedish economist calls for stronger world economic integration which would allow the poor, underdeveloped nations to receive a greater share of the world's benefits. The present system needs to be modified because the disparity between rich and poor nations is becoming greater. Although economic aid may help rectify this imbalance, the poor states need to join together to establish a stronger political base, while international organizations need to play a more dominant role.

Perkins, J.O.N. INTERNATIONAL POLICY FOR THE WORLD ECONOMY. London: George Allen & Unwin, 1969. 232 p.

Examines some of the important international economic issues on which states will be required to cooperate in the future if world economic harmony is to prevail. Issues analyzed include international monetary arrangements, trade policies, regional integration, and economic assistance.

Prochnow, Herbert V., ed. WORLD ECONOMIC PROBLEMS AND POLICIES. New York: Harper & Row, 1965. 382 p.

These articles discuss regional and international economic issues and problems of the early 1960s.

Schmitt, Hans O. "Integration and Conflict in the World Economy." JOURNAL OF COMMON MARKET STUDIES 8 (September 1969): 1-18.

Schwarzenberger, Georg. ECONOMIC WORLD ORDER? Manchester, Engl.: Manchester University Press, 1970. xii, 153 p.

A compilation of five lectures given at the University of Manchester on the theme: "Does an effective world order exist on which international economic law may securely rest?" The author's legal and institutional analysis of the world system leads him to the conclusion that the world order has a weak consensual basis and that there is no firm basis for international economic law.

Strange, Susan. "The Meaning of Multilateral Surveillance." In THE POLITICS OF INTERNATIONAL ORGANIZATIONS, edited by Robert W. Cox, pp. 231-347. New York: Praeger Publishers, 1970.

A provocative essay on the political dimensions of international debtor-creditor relations. Questions the assumption that the creditors automatically have complete control over debtors. Strange argues that many of the nineteenth-century tools for debt collection are no longer available and for this reason multilateral agencies are becoming more important in the process of debt repayment.

Tinbergen, Jan. "Building a World Order." In ECONOMICS AND WORLD ORDER: FROM THE 1970'S TO THE 1990'S, edited by Jagdish N. Bhagwati, pp. 141-56. New York: Macmillan Co., 1972.

Tinbergen, a Nobel laureate economist, calls for institutional decision making at the international level in order to control the development of the world more effectively. International planning is essential for maximizing optimal world welfare.

_____. INTERNATIONAL ECONOMIC INTEGRATION. 3d rev. ed. Amsterdam: Elsevier, 1964. 141 p.

The distinguished Dutch economist calls for the strengthening of international organizations which will promote world integration-- a process he believes will provide greater international financial stability and strengthen the economies of the less-developed countries.

_____. SHAPING THE WORLD ECONOMY; SUGGESTIONS FOR AN INTERNATIONAL ECONOMIC POLICY. New York: Twentieth Century Fund, 1962. 330 p.

Various policy recommendations are set forth for strengthening the world economy. Tinbergen's suggestions flow from a concern for the economic development of the poor nations and for increasing the financial stability of the world through stronger international economic integration.

Viner, Jacob. "Power versus Plenty as Objectives of Foreign Policy in the Seventeenth and Eighteenth Centuries." WORLD POLITICS 1 (October 1948): 1-29.

B. INTERNATIONAL ECONOMIC INSTITUTIONS

Alexandrowicz, Charles H. WORLD ECONOMIC AGENCIES: LAW AND PRACTICE. New York: Praeger Publishers, 1962. 310 p.

An excellent institutional analysis of the principal international organizations concerned with world economic issues. The study examines the IMF, the World Bank, GATT, as well as selected international commodity agencies.

Aubrey, Henry G. ATLANTIC ECONOMIC COOPERATION: THE CASE OF THE OECD. Published for the Council on Foreign Relations. New York: Praeger Publishers, 1967. 211 p.

An institutional analysis of the OECD as an instrument for facilitating economic cooperation among the members of the Atlantic Community.

Baldwin, David A. "The International Bank in Political Perspective." WORLD POLITICS 18 (October 1965): 68-81.

A study of the political dimensions of the World Bank. Baldwin suggests that the Bank is political in three respects: its allocation of money, the impact of loans on countries, and the influence of the Bank on governments.

_____. "The International Development Association: Theory and Practice." ECONOMIC DEVELOPMENT AND CULTURAL CHANGE 10 (October 1966): 86-96.

A study of the politics of the establishment and operation of the IDA.

Blair, Patricia W. "The Dimension of Poverty." INTERNATIONAL ORGANIZATION 23 (Summer 1969): 683-709.

A general discussion of the problem of world poverty and what international organizations can do to help alleviate such conditions.

Bleicher, Samuel A. "UN vs. IBRD: A Dilemma of Functionalism." INTERNATIONAL ORGANIZATION 24 (Winter 1970): 32-47.

An analysis of the dispute between the United Nations and the World Bank over the latter's refusal to deny economic privileges to Portugal and South Africa for their alleged apartheid policies.

Cordovez, Diego. UNCTAD AND DEVELOPMENT DIPLOMACY; FROM CONFRONTATION TO STRATEGY. Middlesex, Engl.: Journal of World Trade Law Publishers, n.d. 165 p.

A study of the institutional development of the United Nations Conference on Trade and Development and the role such an organization plays in world politics. Chapter 7 examines the politics of the UNCTAD meetings at Geneva in 1964 and at New Delhi in 1968.

Cox, Robert W., and Jacobson, Harold, eds. THE ANATOMY OF INFLUENCE: DECISION-MAKING IN INTERNATIONAL ORGANIZATIONS. New Haven, Conn.: Yale University Press, 1973. xiii, 497 p.

The political decision-making process within the following eight organizations is examined: International Telecommunications Union, International Labor Organization, UNESCO, World Health Organization, International Atomic Energy Agency, International Monetary Fund, GATT, and UNCTAD. The studies focus on the participants of the organizations and their sources and methods of influence.

Curzon, Gerard. "The General Agreement on Tariffs and Trade: Pressures and Strategies for Task Expansion." In THE POLITICS OF INTERNATIONAL ORGANIZATIONS, edited by Robert W. Cox, pp. 248-57. New York: Praeger Publishers, 1970.

> A short, useful essay on the political economy of GATT. Curzon argues that technical, economic considerations are the primary factors dictating the expansion of this organization, although political forces may exert some influence, as was the case with the expansion of GATT to include the Eastern bloc states.

Dam, Kenneth W. THE GATT-LAW AND INTERNATIONAL ECONOMIC ORGANIZATION. Chicago: University of Chicago Press, 1970. xvii, 480 p.

Dell, Sidney. "An Appraisal on UNCTAD III." WORLD DEVELOPMENT 1 (May 1973): 1-13.

_____. THE INTER-AMERICAN DEVELOPMENT BANK; A STUDY IN DEVELOPMENT FINANCING. New York: Praeger Publishers, 1972. xv, 255 p.

> A study of the origins, organization, programs, and impact of the Inter-American Development Bank.

Esman, Milton J., and Cheever, Daniel S. THE COMMON AID EFFORT: THE DEVELOPMENT ASSISTANCE ACTIVITIES OF THE ORGANIZATION FOR ECONOMIC COOPERATION AND DEVELOPMENT. Columbus: Ohio State University Press, 1967. 421 p.

Friedeberg, A.S. THE UNITED NATIONS CONFERENCE ON TRADE AND DEVELOPMENT OF 1964: THE THEORY OF THE PERIPHERAL ECONOMY AT THE CENTRE OF INTERNATIONAL POLITICAL DISCUSSIONS. Rotterdam, Netherlands: Rotterdam University Press, 1969. xv, 235 p.

Gardner, Richard N., and Millikan, Max, eds. THE GLOBAL PARTNERSHIP; INTERNATIONAL AGENCIES AND ECONOMIC DEVELOPMENT. New York: Praeger Publishers, 1968. 498 p.

> These essays, published earlier in INTERNATIONAL ORGANIZATION, describe the functions and operations of international organizations designed to promote economic growth and facilitate world trade.

Gosovic, Branislav. UNCTAD: CONFLICT AND COMPROMISE. Leiden, Netherlands: A.W. Sijthoff, 1972. 334 p.

> This study, one of the most thorough and complete analyses of UNCTAD, traces the historical development of the organization and examines the areas of trade and development where UNCTAD has sought to develop concensus among the LDCs. The last part of the volume deals with the institutional development of UNCTAD and its relationship to other international organizations.

Gregg, Robert W. "U.N. Regional Commissions and Integration in the Under-developed Regions." INTERNATIONAL ORGANIZATION 20 (Spring 1966): 208-32.

> Examines the role each of the three U.N. regional commissions has had in promoting regional integration. Gregg suggests that the U.N. Commissions for Latin America (ECLA), the Far East (ECAFE), and Africa (ECA) have had, respectively, a moderate, low, and marginal impact on the integration of their regions.

Hagras, Kamal M. UNITED NATIONS CONFERENCE ON TRADE AND DE-VELOPMENT; A CASE STUDY IN U.N. DIPLOMACY. New York: Praeger Publishers, 1965. xiii, 171 p.

> A case study of the first UNCTAD conference held in Geneva in 1964. The investigation is undertaken within the framework of international organizations and their role in the international system.

Herrera, Felipe. "The Inter-American Development Bank and Latin American Integration Movement." JOURNAL OF COMMON MARKET STUDIES 5 (December 1966): 172-80.

Krause, Lawrence B., and Nye, Joseph S., Jr. "Reflections on the Economics and Politics of International Economic Organizations." INTERNATIONAL ORGANIZATION 29 (Winter 1975): 323-42.

> The authors suggest that the traditional tools of political science and economics must be adapted to the problems of the international system if there is to be a clearer understanding of economic organizations. The analysis of these institutions should focus on their role in promoting efficiency--an economic concern, and on security--a political concern.

Lagos, Gustavo. "The Political Role of Regional Economic Organizations in Latin America." JOURNAL OF COMMON MARKET STUDIES 6 (June 1968): 291-309.

> Examines the political influence of Latin American regional economic organizations on the formulation and development of Latin American integration.

Laves, Walter H.C. "Political Development Assistance by United Nations Organizations." In THE POLITICS OF INTERNATIONAL ORGANIZATIONS, edited by Robert W. Cox, pp. 117-27. New York: Praeger Publishers, 1970.

> Attempts to determine how U.N. organizations can exert influence on states. Several suggestions are offered on how international organizations can increase their influence in developing countries.

Lewis, John P., and Kapur, Ishan, eds. THE WORLD BANK GROUP: MUL-
TILATERAL AID AND THE 1970'S. Lexington, Mass.: D.C. Heath & Co.,
1973. xvii, 168 p.

> Papers and proceedings of a seminar held in 1971 at the Woodrow
> Wilson School of Public and International Affairs, Princeton Uni-
> versity, on the future role of the World Bank. The essays ex-
> amine primarily the economic functions and processes of the Bank's
> aid programs.

Mason, Edward [S.], and Asher, Robert [E.]. THE WORLD BANK SINCE
BRETTON WOODS. Washington, D.C.: Brookings Institution, 1973. 915 p.

> The definitive study of the World Bank. It examines the origins,
> policies, operations, and impact of the Bank and its subsidiary
> organizations--the International Finance Corporation, the Interna-
> tional Development Association, and the International Center for
> Settlement of Investment Disputes. Part 3 analyzes the Bank's
> "international diplomacy."

Matecki, Bronislaw. ESTABLISHMENT OF THE INTERNATIONAL FINANCE
CORPORATION AND UNITED STATES POLICY; A CASE STUDY IN INTERNA-
TIONAL ORGANIZATION. New York: Praeger Publishers, 1957. 194 p.

Meerhaeghe, M.A.G. van. INTERNATIONAL ECONOMIC INSTITUTIONS.
2d ed. London: Longman Group, 1971. xxvii, 381 p.

> A study of the structure and functions of the major international
> and regional economic organizations.

Mundell, Robert A. "The International Monetary Fund." JOURNAL OF
WORLD TRADE LAW 3 (September-October 1969): 455-98.

Ohlin, Goran. "The Organization for Economic Cooperation and Development."
INTERNATIONAL ORGANIZATION 22 (Winter 1968): 231-43.

Oppenheim, V.H. "Whose World Bank?" FOREIGN POLICY 19 (Summer
1975): 99-108.

> A discussion of some of the emerging tensions over the relations
> between the OPEC countries and the World Bank.

Reid, Escott. "McNamara's World Bank." FOREIGN AFFAIRS 51 (July 1973):
794-810.

Richards, J.H. INTERNATIONAL ECONOMIC INSTITUTIONS. New York:
Holt, Rinehart and Winston, 1970. 318 p.

> A good, up-to-date undergraduate text on the international or-
> ganizations dealing with economic development and trade.

Singh, Lalita P. THE POLITICS OF ECONOMIC COOPERATION IN ASIA: A STUDY OF ASIAN INTERNATIONAL ORGANIZATIONS. Columbia: University of Missouri Press, 1966. xiii, 271 p.

Siotis, J. "The Secretariat of the U.N. Economic Commission for Europe and the First 10 Years." INTERNATIONAL ORGANIZATION 19 (Spring 1965): 177-202.

Weaver, James H. THE INTERNATIONAL DEVELOPMENT ASSOCIATION; A NEW APPROACH TO FOREIGN AID. New York: Praeger Publishers, 1965. 268 p.

> A study of the origins and development of the IDA and its role in the economic development of the LDCs. U.S. policy toward the development and operation of the association is examined.

White, John [A.]. REGIONAL DEVELOPMENT BANKS, A STUDY. London: Overseas Development Institute, 1970. 204 p.

Wightman, David. ECONOMIC COOPERATION IN EUROPE. Published for the Carnegie Endowment. New York: Praeger Publishers, 1957. 288 p.

> A descriptive study of the operations of the U.N. Economic Commission for Europe up to 1954.

_____. TOWARD ECONOMIC COOPERATION IN ASIA: THE UNITED NATIONS COMMISSION FOR ASIA AND THE FAR EAST. New Haven, Conn.: Yale University Press, 1963. xii, 400 p.

C. U.S. ECONOMIC RELATIONS

Bergsten, C. Fred. "The Threat From the Third World." FOREIGN POLICY 11 (Summer 1973): 102-24.

> U.S. economic policy neglects LDCs almost entirely. Because of the increasingly important role of the Third World in the world system, and because of the specific importance of many of these states as sources of primary products, the United States should establish a more deliberate, cooperative policy with these states, giving them trade preferences and untying economic aid.

Bidwell, Percy W. RAW MATERIALS: A STUDY OF AMERICAN POLICY. Published for the Council on Foreign Relations. New York: Harper and Brothers, 1958. 403 p.

> Although out of date, this study remains one of the most careful examinations of U.S. postwar trade policies toward primary products.

Calleo, David P., and Rowland, Benjamin M. AMERICA AND THE WORLD POLITICAL ECONOMY: ATLANTIC DREAMS AND NATIONAL REALITIES. Bloomington: Indiana University Press, 1973. 360 p.

The authors trace the development of the Atlantic Community ideal—an ideal of strong interdependent, democratic nations joined together through the principles of free trade and federalism—and examine some of its shortcomings as a foundation for relations within the community itself and between the community and Japan and the LDCs. The writers believe that the traditional ideal should be replaced by a liberal, plural system where political hegemony is made unnecessary.

Cohen, Benjamin J., ed. AMERICAN FOREIGN ECONOMIC POLICY: ESSAYS AND COMMENTS. New York: Harper & Row, 1968. 439 p.

A useful set of readings covering four major issues: the international economic framework, the relations between industrial states, East-West economic relations, and economic relations with the LDCs. The introduction is an excellent short analysis of the underlying principles of American foreign economic policy.

Diebold, William, Jr. "Economic Aspects of an Atlantic Community." INTERNATIONAL ORGANIZATION 17 (Summer 1963): 663-82.

A general overview of the economic forces operating within Western Europe as well as within the broader Atlantic Community.

_____. "The Future of United States Foreign Economic Policy." INTERNATIONAL JOURNAL 29 (Autumn 1974): 557-76.

Gardner, Lloyd C. ECONOMIC ASPECTS OF NEW DEAL DIPLOMACY. Madison: University of Wisconsin Press, 1964. 409 p.

An economic history of U.S. foreign economic policy of the 1930s and early 1940s.

Gardner, Richard H. IN PURSUIT OF WORLD ORDER: U.S. FOREIGN POLICY AND INTERNATIONAL ORGANIZATIONS. New York: Praeger Publishers, 1964. 263 p.

A study of the role of international organizations as agents of world peace and economic well-being. The underlying theme of the volume is that multilateral cooperation through international organizations serves the U.S. national interest better than other alternative policies.

_____. STERLING-DOLLAR DIPLOMACY; ANGLO-AMERICAN COLLABORATION IN THE RECONSTRUCTION OF MULTILATERAL TRADE. Oxford: Clarendon Press, 1956. xxii, 432 p.

A political history of U.S.-British economic relations during the postwar era. The study deals specifically with the Anglo-American role in the creation of multilateral economic agencies.

_____, ed. BLUEPRINT FOR PEACE; BEING THE PROPOSALS OF PROMINENT AMERICANS TO THE WHITE HOUSE CONFERENCE ON INTERNATIONAL CO-OPERATION. New York: McGraw-Hill Book Co., 1966. 404 p.

A collection of sixteen committee reports prepared by participants at the 1965 White House Conference on International Cooperation. Chapters 8, 9, and 10 deal with economic aid, international finance, and world trade, respectively.

Harris, Seymour E., ed. FOREIGN ECONOMIC POLICY FOR THE UNITED STATES. Cambridge, Mass.: Harvard University Press, 1948. 490 p.

An important collection of readings on different dimensions of U.S. economic policies during the immediate postwar era.

Lerche, Charles O., Jr. FOREIGN POLICY OF THE AMERICAN PEOPLE. 2d ed. Englewood Cliffs, N.J.: Prentice-Hall, 1961. 489 p.

Chapter 14 of this introductory text examines the economic dimensions of U.S. foreign policy. Three themes are discussed: the cost of foreign policy, the cost of aid, and the cost of trade.

McKitterick, Nathaniel. EAST-WEST TRADE; THE BACKGROUND OF U.S. POLICY. New York: Twentieth Century Fund, 1966. 59 p.

Malmgren, Harald B. "Managing Foreign Economic Policy." FOREIGN POLICY 6 (Spring 1972): 42-68.

The United States does not have a coherent, consistent foreign economic policy, mainly because there is no effective institutional structure assigned to develop such policy. The author argues for a complete restructuring of the Department of State.

McLellan, David S., and Woodhouse, Charles E. "The Business Elite and Foreign Policy." WESTERN POLITICAL QUARTERLY 13 (March 1960): 172-90.

An analysis of foreign policy perspectives of U.S. businessmen. The views of the business elite are based on Congressional testimony toward six postwar issues: the Bretton Woods Agreements Act and the British Loan Agreements, the European Recovery Program, Point Four, the Mutual Security Program, the International Finance Corporation, and the Development Loan Fund.

_____. "Businessmen in Foreign Policy." SOUTHWESTERN SOCIAL SCIENCE QUARTERLY 39 (March 1959): 283-90.

The authors examine the professional backgrounds of government employees in key foreign policy-making posts during three separate periods. They conclude that "the most significant trend in the profile of foreign policy decision-making is the importance assumed by business and financial figures."

Maynes, Charles W., Jr. "Who Pays for Foreign Policy?" FOREIGN POL-ICY 15 (Summer 1974): 152-68.

A general, nonquantitative analysis of the relationship between domestic economic interests and foreign policy. Maynes attempts to determine some of the positive and negative effects of particular foreign policy issues on specific groups of Americans.

Mikesell, Raymond F. U.S. ECONOMIC POLICY AND INTERNATIONAL RE-LATIONS. New York: McGraw-Hill Book Co., 1952. 341 p.

A historical account of U.S. economic policy from 1919 to the beginning of the 1950s, with special emphasis on the postwar era. Of particular interest are the chapters on the postwar international monetary and investment policies.

Rosenau, James N., ed. DOMESTIC SOURCES OF FOREIGN POLICY. New York: Free Press, 1967. xiv, 340 p.

The essays, originally given at a conference on public opinion and foreign policy, examine domestic political and sociological sources of the U.S. foreign policy-making process. Some of the issues examined include attitudes, social position, voting behavior, and urbanization.

Salant, Walter S., et al. THE UNITED STATES BALANCE OF PAYMENTS in 1968. Washington, D.C.: Brookings Institution, 1963. 298 p.

A meticulous analysis of the U.S. balance of payments system with a view of assessing the probable impact of major future develop-ments on it. Some of the domestic and international forces ex-amined in terms of their balance of payments effects include the EEC, private foreign investment, foreign aid, defense expenditures, and industrial competitiveness.

Spanier, John W. AMERICAN FOREIGN POLICY SINCE WORLD WAR II. 6th ed. New York: Praeger Publishers, 1973. 295 p.

An excellent, concise analytic history of contemporary foreign re-lations of the United States.

Stark, John R. "International Economic Policy--Perspectives for the 1970's." JOURNAL OF INTERNATIONAL LAW AND ECONOMICS 5 (January 1971): 101-20.

A discussion of some of the major economic issues the United States will have to deal with in the 1970s.

Steel, Ronald. IMPERIALISTS AND OTHER HEROES; A CHRONICLE OF THE AMERICAN EMPIRE. New York: Random House, 1971. 447 p.

A series of previously published articles on postwar American for-eign policy. The essays are journalistic in style and the tone is generally critical of the political and economic dimensions of U.S. policy. Steel is particularly critical of the inconsistencies between objectives and implementation of U.S. policy.

Wagner, R. Harrison. UNITED STATES POLICY TOWARD LATIN AMERICA: A STUDY IN DOMESTIC AND INTERNATIONAL POLITICS. Stanford, Calif.: Stanford University Press, 1970. 246 p.

The foreign policy-making process is a complex one that is influenced not only by competing domestic interests but also by the realities of the international system. Wagner suggests that simplistic explanations of U.S. foreign economic policy toward Latin America do not stand up under careful scrutiny. This study is probably the most balanced explanation of U.S. postwar economic policy toward Latin America.

Westerfield, H. Bradford. THE INSTRUMENTS OF AMERICA'S FOREIGN POLICY. New York: Thomas Y. Crowell Co., 1963. 538 p.

A general historical text on the postwar foreign policy of the United States. Chapters 13-19 examine selected issues and dimensions of American economic policies.

Williams, Benjamin H. ECONOMIC FOREIGN POLICY OF THE UNITED STATES. New York: Howard Fertig, 1967. 410 p.

Originally published in 1929, this study examines the early twentieth-century economic policy of the United States. The historical account deals primarily with foreign investment and commercial policy.

Wilson, Joan Hoff. AMERICAN BUSINESS AND FOREIGN POLICY, 1920-1933. Lexington: University Press of Kentucky, 1971. 339 p.

A historical account of the role of the American business community in U.S. foreign economic policies during the Republican administrations following the First World War. The study examines the following foreign policy issues: disarmament, allied war debts and German reparations, Latin America, and the Far East. Extensive notes included.

Wolf, Charles, Jr. UNITED STATES POLICY AND THE THIRD WORLD: PROBLEMS AND ANALYSIS. Boston: Little, Brown and Co., 1967. 204 p.

A valuable collection of analytical essays on American foreign policy toward the LDCs. Chapters 5 and 6 analyze the statistical relationship between military expenditures and democracy in Latin American countries. Chapter 9 discusses the relationship of military aid to economic assistance.

Woodrow Wilson Foundation. THE POLITICAL ECONOMY OF AMERICAN FOREIGN POLICY. New York: Henry Holt and Co., 1955. 414 p.

101678

A remarkably prescient study of U.S. foreign economic policy prepared by a group of nine distinguished scholars. Although there is useful historical data on nineteenth- and twentieth-century international economic systems (chapters 1 and 6), most of the materials focus on U.S. trade and development policy concerns of the early 1950s. Many of the insights and policy implications are still valid.

D. OTHER BILATERAL ECONOMIC RELATIONS

Alba, Victor. ALLIANCE WITHOUT ALLIES: MYTHOLOGY OF PROGRESS IN LATIN AMERICA. New York: Praeger Publishers, 1965. 224 p.

A critique of Latin American social structure and of the limited scope of social reform contemplated by the Alliance for Progress.

Alnaswari, Abbas. "The Collective Bargaining Power of Oil Producing Countries." JOURNAL OF WORLD TRADE LAW 7 (March-April 1973): 188-207.

Written before the success of the OPEC oil price increase of 1973, the author maintains that the collective bargaining power of Arab oil-producing states is weak and that it will continue to play a marginal role in the future international oil economy.

Bachmann, Hans. THE EXTERNAL RELATIONS OF LESS-DEVELOPED COUNTRIES; A MANUAL OF ECONOMIC POLICIES. New York: Praeger Publishers, 1968. xix, 341 p.

"The main purpose of this book is to present to the governments of less-developed countries and the students of development problems a comprehensive manual on the questions and tasks which confront these governments in the field of external economic relations and to provide a description and analysis of the possible solutions to these problems." A large portion of the study is devoted to commercial and monetary policy.

Broadbridge, Seymour, and Collick, Martin. "Japan's International Policies: Political and Economic Motivations." INTERNATIONAL AFFAIRS 44 (April 1968): 240-53.

Bryant, William E. JAPANESE PRIVATE ECONOMIC DIPLOMACY; AN ANALYSIS OF BUSINESS-GOVERNMENT LINKAGES. New York: Praeger Publishers, 1975. xiv, 138 p.

A study of the political economy of Japan's international economic relations, focusing on the role of businessmen in developing and improving the foreign economic climate for Japan.

Child, Sarah. POVERTY AND AFFLUENCE: AN INTRODUCTION TO THE INTERNATIONAL RELATIONS OF RICH AND POOR ECONOMIES. London:

H. Hamilton, 1968. 208 p.

The first part of this study examines the development of the contemporary international economic system, while the second part focuses on relevant economic issues of the 1950s and 1960s, such as aid, trade, commodity agreements, and international monetary reform.

Diaz-Alejandro, Carlos F. "North-South Relations: The Economic Component." INTERNATIONAL ORGANIZATION 29 (Winter 1975): 213-42.

Dreier, John C., ed. THE ALLIANCE FOR PROGRESS: PROBLEMS AND PERSPECTIVES. Baltimore: Johns Hopkins Press, 1962. xviii, 146 p.

A group of five essays on the politics and economics of the Alliance for Progress by noted North and South American statesmen.

Finley, David D. "A Political Perspective of Economic Relations in the Communist Camp." WESTERN POLITICAL QUARTERLY 17 (June 1964): 294-316.

Geiger, Theodore. THE CONFLICTED RELATIONSHIP: THE WEST AND THE TRANSFORMATION OF ASIA, AFRICA AND LATIN AMERICA. Published for the Council on Foreign Relations. New York: McGraw-Hill Book Co., 1967. xiv, 303 p.

Holzman, Franklyn D., and Legvold, Robert. "The Economics and Politics of East-West Relations." INTERNATIONAL ORGANIZATION 29 (Winger 1965): 275-322.

Johnson, Harry G. ECONOMIC POLICIES TOWARD LESS DEVELOPED COUNTRIES. New York: Praeger Publishers, 1968. 271 p.

Written in large measure to deal with some of the economic issues raised at the 1964 United Nations Conference on Trade and Development (UNCTAD), this study remains one of the best analytical, dispassionate studies of economic policies toward the LDCs. Johnson examines aid and foreign investment, but most of his attention is given to commercial policy and more specifically to the trade policies that might be utilized to help developing countries. In chapter 3, the author provides an excellent analysis of domestic and international policies that impede economic growth.

Kindleberger, Charles P., and Shonfield, Andrew, eds. NORTH AMERICAN AND WESTERN EUROPEAN ECONOMIC POLICIES. London: Macmillan & Co.; New York: St. Martin's Press, 1971. xxiv, 551 p.

Proceedings of a conference sponsored by the International Economic Association.

Levinson, Jerome, and Onis, Juan de. THE ALLIANCE THAT LOST ITS WAY; A CRITICAL REPORT ON THE ALLIANCE FOR PROGRESS. Chicago: Quadrangle Books, 1970. xi, 381 p.

Lodgaard, Sverre. "On the Relationship Between East-West Economic Cooperation and Political Change in Eastern Europe." JOURNAL OF PEACE RESEARCH 11 (1974): 325-40.

> Given the increasing amount of economic cooperation between East and West, the author argues that the Western economic concepts and technology are ineluctably influencing not only the economies of Eastern European states but also the social and political forces of these nations. Trade and investment are instruments of domestic political change.

Masnata, Albert. EAST-WEST ECONOMIC CO-OPERATION. Translated from the French by John Cuthbert-Brown. Farnsborough, Engl.: Saxon House; Lexington, Mass.: Lexington Books, 1974. 144 p.

> Discusses some of the major obstacles between free-market and state-controlled economies and sets forth policy guidelines on how to improve East-West economic cooperation.

Ojedokun, Olasupo. "The Changing Pattern of Nigeria's International Economic Relations: The Decline of the Colonial Nexus, 1960-1966." JOURNAL OF THE DEVELOPING AREAS 6 (July 1972): 535-54.

Powelson, John P. "The International Politics of Latin American Economics." In INTERNATIONAL ECONOMICS AND DEVELOPMENT; ESSAYS IN HONOR OF RAUL PREBISCH, edited by Luis E. DiMarco, pp. 429-43. New York: Academic Press, 1972.

> Powelson suggests that the underlying theories of Latin American international economic relations have had a negative political impact on the United States. The theories, developed largely by the U.N. Economic Commission for Latin America, have stressed the weakness and powerlessness of the poor states and the need for grants and trade preferences. Powelson suggests that Latin American countries should adopt a "policy of strength."

Preeg, Ernest H. ECONOMIC BLOCS AND U.S. FOREIGN POLICY. Washington, D.C.: National Planning Association, 1974. 202 p.

> Examines the major postwar developments in the international economic system and evaluates how well the United States, Western Europe, and Japan have adapted to the new economic environment. Chapter 9 is an analysis of the politics of international economic relations.

Rosenbaum, H. Jon, and Tyler, William G. "South-South Relations: The Economic and Political Content of Interactions Among Developing Countries." IN-

TERNATIONAL ORGANIZATION 29 (Winter 1975): 243-74.

Schertz, Lyle P. "World Food Prices and the Poor." FOREIGN AFFAIRS 52 (April 1974): 511-37.

> An analysis of the production and distribution of food and the prob-
> lems posed by the shortages of the early 1970s. Schertz argues that the
> developed countries should reexamine their food policies so that the
> needs of the poor states might be met more effectively.

Wallace, William. "The Management of Foreign Economic Policy in Britain." INTERNATIONAL AFFAIRS 50 (April 1967): 251-67.

> Provides a brief overview of the foreign economic policy-making
> process of Britain and some of the issues and problems related to
> British foreign economic relations.

Waverman, Leonard. "Oil and the Distribution of International Power." IN-TERNATIONAL JOURNAL 29 (Autumn 1974): 619-35.

> Argues that the oil crisis of 1973 and 1974 will not shift power
> from the West to the East but may instead strengthen the power
> of the West even more. Within the Western industrial states, the
> United States will gain at the expense of Europe and Japan.

Wiles, P.J.D. COMMUNIST INTERNATIONAL ECONOMICS. New York: Praeger Publishers, 1968. 566 p.

> The definitive study of Soviet bloc international economic theory
> and practice in the postwar era. See particularly chapters 12,
> 16, and 17 on "The Political Economy of International Integration,"
> "The Economic Theory of Economic War and Imperialism," and "Eco-
> nomic Warfare in Communist Practice."

Zaubermann, A. "Gold in Soviet Economic Theory and Politics." AMERICAN ECONOMIC REVIEW 40 (December 1951): 879-90.

Zyzniewski, Stanley J. "Soviet Foreign Economic Policy." POLITICAL SCI-ENCE QUARTERLY 73 (June 1958): 206-33.

> An analysis of the Soviet Union's postwar economic policy, with
> emphasis on the international dimensions of that policy.

Chapter 3

POLITICS AND TRADE

Trade is the process by which countries buy and sell goods from other states. If trade were completely free--that is, if goods could move across national boundaries without restrictions--then trade would be a purely economic phenomenon. In practice, however, governments establish policies designed to limit and control the purchase and sale of products between nations. The most common trade restriction is the tariff, the imposition of a duty on foreign goods entering a state's boundaries. Other means of controlling trade include cartels, commodity agreements, boycotts, and embargoes. A cartel is an economic association of sellers cooperating together to limit competition in order to stabilize or increase prices. Commodity agreements attempt to achieve similar objectives through governmental accords. A boycott is an attempt to prohibit foreign imports from particular states or regions, while an embargo attempts to prohibit shipment of goods to particular areas.

Politics relates to trade at two different levels. At the domestic level, national political forces will exert influence on the development of foreign trade policies in accordance with the competing interests of different economic and political groups. At the international level, foreign economic interests will seek to limit and control foreign economic interests of other states, particularly when states are pursuing similar objectives. Since trade policy must be implemented within the international system, states must take into account the trade policies of other states and, where they conflict, must seek to reconcile differences through negotiation. The development and implementation of foreign economic policies thus involves domestic and international politics.

A. GENERAL COMMERCIAL RELATIONS

Alker, Hayward, Jr., and Puchala, Donald. "Trends in Economic Partnership: The North Atlantic Area, 1928-1963." In QUANTITATIVE INTERNATIONAL POLITICS: INSIGHTS AND EVIDENCE, edited by J. David Singer, pp. 287-316. New York: Free Press, 1968. 394 p.

> An empirical investigation of trade relations in the North Atlantic area from 1928 to 1963 with a view of drawing political im-

plications from such analysis.

Allen, Robert L. "Economic Motives in Soviet Foreign Trade Policy." SOUTH-
ERN ECONOMIC JOURNAL 25 (October 1958): 189-201.

Alting Von Geusau, Frans A.M., ed. ECONOMIC RELATIONS AFTER THE
KENNEDY ROUND. Leiden, Netherlands: A.S. Sijthoff, 1969. 224 p.

> This collection of articles, prepared for an international colloquium
> at the John F. Kennedy Institute of Tilburg, Netherlands, examines
> different issues and concerns of the Kennedy Round of Trade Nego-
> tiations.

Balassa, Bela. TRADE LIBERALIZATION AMONG INDUSTRIAL COUNTRIES:
OBJECTIVES AND ALTERNATIVES. Published for the Council on Foreign Relations. New York: McGraw-Hill Book Co., 1967. xvi, 251 p.

> A study of the issues and problems of economic trade among the
> industrial states of the North Atlantic region. Chapter 2 examines
> the political considerations involved in trade liberalization.

Baldwin, Robert E., and Kay, David A. "International Trade and International
Relations." INTERNATIONAL ORGANIZATION 29 (Winter 1975): 99-131.

> The authors examine the existing trade arrangements and then pre-
> sent and evaluate three alternative systems of trade liberalization--
> through the elimination of discriminatory practices, the develop-
> ment of regional trading systems, and the consolidation of the pres-
> ent system.

Bauer, Raymond A.; Pool, Ithiel de Sola; and Dexter, Lewis Anthony. AMERI-
CAN BUSINESS AND PUBLIC POLICY; THE POLITICS OF FOREIGN TRADE.
2d ed. Chicago: Aldine-Atherton, 1972. 490 p.

> A landmark study on the domestic political sources of U.S. foreign
> trade policy from 1953 to 1962. The analysis focuses on the role
> of five groups: individual businessmen, individual firms, the gen-
> eral public, trade associations and lobbies, and the Congress.
> This study, based on extensive empirical data, suggests that the
> relationship between American business and public policy is more
> complex than has generally been thought before, for business firms
> do not all pursue the same interests, nor do they seek similar ob-
> jectives in the same way. A valuable source for public opinion
> data on trade policy.

Cooper, Richard N. "Trade Policy is Foreign Policy." FOREIGN POLICY 9
(Winter 1972-73): 18-36.

> The Yale economist suggests that separation of trade policy from
> foreign policy is no longer tenable. Because international econom-
> ic issues are of central importance in the international relations

of major industrial states, trade policy must be integrated into the whole foreign policy network if there is to be consistency.

Diebold, William, Jr. "U.S. Trade Policy: The New Political Dimensions." FOREIGN AFFAIRS 58 (April 1974): 472-96.

Examines the domestic and international political forces influencing contemporary U.S. trade policies.

Evans, Douglas. THE POLITICS OF TRADE; THE EVOLUTION OF THE SUPER-BLOC. London: Macmillan & Co., 1974. 128 p.

A descriptive account of how the political interests of the super-blocs (the United States, the European Community, the Soviet Union, Japan, and China) have helped shape the international economic system of the 1970s. The study deals primarily with trade and the monetary system.

Feld, Werner J. "Trade Between the U.S. and the European Community: Differing Expectations in a Changing Power Relationship." JOURNAL OF INTERNATIONAL AFFAIRS 28 (1974): 7-24.

Feller, Peter Buck. "The International Antidumping Code--The Confrontation and Accomodation of Independent Executive and Legislative Powers in the Regulation of Foreign Commerce." JOURNAL OF INTERNATIONAL LAW AND ECONOMICS 5 (January 1971): 121-38.

A useful case study on the political basis of foreign economic policy making. The study focuses on the dynamics between the U.S. Congress and the President in the development of a policy on dumping (the selling of goods abroad at prices lower than those on the national market).

Gift, Richard E. "Trading in a Threat System: The U.S.-Soviet Case." JOURNAL OF CONFLICT RESOLUTION 13 (December 1969): 418-37.

A sophisticated analysis of the rational policy alternatives for economic trade between two opposing military powers. The aim of the article is to develop a rational trade model that takes into account the negative political tensions between the two parties.

Hawkins, Harry C., and Norwood, Janet L. "The Legislative Basis of United States Commercial Policy." In STUDIES IN UNITED STATES COMMERCIAL POLICY, edited by William B. Kelly, Jr., pp. 69-123. Chapel Hill: University of North Carolina Press, 1963.

A study of the legal framework of U.S. commercial policy, from the 1934 Trade Agreements Act through the early 1960s.

Hollerman, Leon. JAPAN'S DEPENDENCE ON THE WORLD ECONOMY: THE APPROACH TOWARD ECONOMIC LIBERALIZATION. Princeton, N.J.: Princeton University Press, 1967. 291 p.

Hunsberger, Warren S. JAPAN AND THE UNITED STATES IN WORLD TRADE. Published for the Council on Foreign Relations. New York: Harper & Row, 1964. 494 p.

Kaser, Michael. "Soviet Trade Turns to Europe." FOREIGN POLICY 19 (Summer 1975): 123-35.

> Examines the strengthening of the Soviet Union's commercial relations with Europe during the 1972-75 period.

Krause, Walter, and Mathis, F. John. "The U.S. Policy Shift on East-West Trade." JOURNAL OF INTERNATIONAL AFFAIRS 28 (1974): 25-37.

Mallery, Otto T. MORE THAN CONQUERORS: BUILDING PEACE ON FAIR TRADE. New York: Harper & Row, 1947. 204 p.

> The road to peace can best be achieved through economic prosperity brought about by free trade. To ensure a free trade system, an international legal system must be established.

Malmgren, Harald B. "Coming Trade Wars? Neo-Mercantilism and Foreign Policy." FOREIGN POLICY 1 (Winter 1970-71): 115-43.

> Discusses the rise of economic nationalism in contemporary international economic relations, and the threat that it poses to a peaceful, cooperative world order.

_____. INTERNATIONAL ECONOMIC PEACEKEEPING IN PHASE II. Published for the Atlantic Council of the United States. New York: Quadrangle Books, 1972. xv, 267 p.

> Analyzes some of the major commercial tensions facing the United States and suggests how some of these problems might be eased or eliminated. Much of the study is devoted to nontariff barriers.

Meier, Gerald M. PROBLEMS OF TRADE POLICY. New York: Oxford University Press, 1973. xv, 288 p.

> A study of trade liberalization, textile import quotas, and regional integration, which makes extensive use of documents to present the political and economic basis of policy development. The material on the domestic politics of U.S. textiles is illuminating.

Mendershausen, Horst. "America's Trade Balance and the International Order." WORLD POLITICS 2 (October 1949): 40-66.

Patterson, Gardner. DISCRIMINATION IN INTERNATIONAL TRADE: THE POLICY ISSUES, 1945-1965. Princeton, N.J.: Princeton University Press, 1966. xiv, 414 p.

The study examines the postwar economic policies of the free-world countries. These policies were designed "to make imports from certain geographic areas easier or less costly than imports from other regions, with the explicit aim of accomplishing thereby some other important and explicit policy objective."

Pisar, Samuel. COEXISTENCE AND COMMERCE; GUIDELINES FOR TRANS-ACTIONS BETWEEN EAST AND WEST. New York: McGraw-Hill Book Co., 1970. xv, 558 p.

Pisar, a lawyer, explores the political, economic, and legal framework for carrying out East-West trade. Chapters 4 and 5, on "Trade as an Instrument of Foreign Policy" and "American Dilemmas in Trade with the East," examine the interrelationship of political and economic concerns of trade.

Preeg, Ernest H. TRADERS AND DIPLOMATS; AN ANALYSIS OF THE KEN-NEDY ROUND OF NEGOTIATIONS UNDER THE GENERAL AGREEMENT ON TARIFFS AND TRADE. Washington, D.C.: Brookings Institution, 1970. xv, 320 p.

A study of the political dynamics of the Kennedy Round of Trade Negotiations.

Pryor, Frederick L. THE COMMUNIST FOREIGN TRADE SYSTEM. Cambridge, Mass.: M.I.T. Press, 1963. 296 p.

A meticulous analysis of the postwar international trade system of the Communist-bloc countries. The focus is on the domestic and international economic concerns relating to trade of the 1950s.

Steel, Ronald, ed. U.S. FOREIGN TRADE POLICY. New York: Wilson Co., 1962. 200 p.

A collection of thirty-five articles on U.S. trade policy developments brought about as a result of the Trade Agreements Act of 1962.

Strackbein, O.R. AMERICAN ENTERPRISE AND FOREIGN TRADE. Washington, D.C.: Public Affairs Press, 1965. 193 p.

Points out the fallacies of free trade and discusses why it is important to maintain control over imports. Essentially, a probusiness analysis of commercial policy.

Streeten, Paul, ed. TRADE STRATEGIES FOR DEVELOPMENT. New York: John Wiley & Sons, 1973. xvi, 375 p.

The articles, originally given at the Ninth Cambridge Conference on Development Problems of September, 1972, focus on trade policy, regional integration, technology, the MNC, and farm products and manufactures as they relate to the economic development of LDCs.

United Nations. Report by the Secretary General of the UNCTAD. TOWARDS A NEW TRADE POLICY FOR DEVELOPMENT. New York: 1964. 125 p.

This study, prepared under the leadership of Raul Prebisch, served as the basis of discussion for the first UNCTAD meeting in Geneva in 1964. The report highlights the major trade problems of the LDCs and suggests new trade policies that will encourage economic development.

Viner, Jacob. DUMPING: A PROBLEM IN INTERNATIONAL TRADE. Chicago: University of Chicago Press, 1923. 343 p.

The classic treatise on dumping--the selling of goods abroad at prices lower than those in the national market.

Wells, Sidney. "The Developing Countries, GATT and UNCTAD." INTERNATIONAL AFFAIRS 45 (January 1969): 64-79.

Assesses the major impact on the developing countries of postwar changes in the international economic system. The focus is on GATT, the Kennedy Round, and UNCTAD I and II.

Wilcox, Clair. A CHARTER FOR WORLD TRADE. New York: Macmillan Co., 1949. 333 p.

An exhaustive examination of the postwar attempts to establish an international trade organization. The study traces the historical development of the movement and discusses the major issues and problems involved in the preparation of the legal charter.

Wilczynski, Joseph. THE ECONOMICS AND POLITICS OF EAST-WEST TRADE. New York: Praeger Publishers, 1969. 395 p.

Despite its title, this study is concerned almost exclusively with the economic dimensions of East-West trade.

Wilkinson, Joe [R.]. POLITICS AND TRADE POLICY. Washington, D.C.: Public Affairs Press, 1960. 146 p.

A political history of the Reciprocal Trade Agreements Program during the 1934-58 period. Wilkinson examines the positions of the two American political parties and shows how their changing views allowed American commercial policy to shift.

Wonnacott, R.J. "The Political Economy of Liberalized Trade." INTERNA-

TIONAL JOURNAL 29 (Autumn 1974): 577-90.

> Both Canada and the United States would benefit economically through the establishment of free trade between them. Since the political problems associated with liberal trade are probably less difficult than is often supposed, Canada should keep this option open for consideration.

Zartman, I. William. THE POLITICS OF TRADE NEGOTIATIONS BETWEEN AFRICA AND THE EUROPEAN COMMUNITY: THE WEAK CONFRONT THE STRONG. Princeton, N.J.: Princeton University Press, 1971. 243 p.

> Explores the nature of North-South diplomacy by analyzing trade negotiations between the European Community and African states.

B. TRADE RESTRICTIONS:
COMMODITY AGREEMENTS AND CARTELS

Adelman, M.A. "Is the Oil Shortage Real? Oil Companies as OPEC Tax Collectors." FOREIGN POLICY 9 (Winter 1972-73): 69-107.

> In this influential but controversial article Adelman asserts that the oil shortage is one that has been contrived by the monopoly power of the OPEC countries.

Bauer, P.T. "Commodity Agreements: Aid or Trade?" INTERNATIONAL JOURNAL 29 (Autumn 1974): 610-18.

> Commodity agreements are not an effective way of transferring resources from the rich to the poor nations because such agreements are regressive and arbitrary. The most effective way of helping a country is through cash grants.

Bergsten, C. Fred. "The Threat is Real." FOREIGN POLICY 14 (Spring 1974): 84-90.

> Suggests that the threat from the raw-material-exporting states of the Third World is a very real one. Based on the success of OPEC, other commodity cartels may be established which would increase prices significantly. Industrialized countries should be prepared to deal with such developments by adopting cooperative policies toward the LDCs.

Boorman, James A. III. "Economic Coercion in International Law: The Arab Oil Weapon and the Ensuing Juridical Issues." JOURNAL OF INTERNATIONAL LAW AND ECONOMICS 9 (August 1974): 205-31.

> Evaluates the legality of the oil embargo of the Arab oil-producing states and finds that it did not violate customary international law, international agreements among participant states, or any pertinent U.N. commitments.

Dam, Kenneth W. "Implementation of Import Quotas: The Case of Oil." JOURNAL OF LAW AND ECONOMICS 14 (April 1971): 1-60.

A comprehensive review of the U.S. oil import quota program, with some evaluation of its effectiveness.

Edwards, Corwin D. CONTROL OF CARTELS AND MONOPOLIES; AN INTERNATIONAL COMPARISON. Dobbs Ferry, N.Y.: Oceana Publications, 1967. viii, 380 p.

Edwards, John. "The International Tin Agreement." JOURNAL OF WORLD TRADE LAW 3 (May-June 1969): 237-50.

Traces the historical evolution of the international tin agreement and the role it has played in controlling the world price of tin. A copy of the Third International Tin Agreement of 1967 is appended.

Fisher, Bart S. THE INTERNATIONAL COFFEE AGREEMENT; A STUDY IN COFFEE DIPLOMACY. New York: Praeger Publishers, 1972. 287 p.

A case study of the politics and economics of the coffee commodity agreement.

Galloway, Thomas L. "The International Coffee Agreement." JOURNAL OF WORLD TRADE LAW 7 (May-June 1973): 354-75.

Examines the effectiveness of the international coffee agreement during the 1960s. Although the cartel experienced a number of difficulties, it managed to help stabilize prices by adjusting long-term supply to long-term demand.

Krasner, Stephen D. "Business Government Relations: The Case of the International Coffee Agreement." INTERNATIONAL ORGANIZATION 27 (Autumn 1973): 495-516.

A case study of the coffee commodity agreement focusing on the role of business in the process of making public policy.

_____. "Manipulating International Commodity Markets: Brazilian Coffee Policy, 1906-1962." PUBLIC POLICY 21 (Fall 1973): 493-524.

On the basis of the Brazilian experience with coffee, Krasner suggests that an LDC producer can exert some control over its international economic environment. To the extent that Brazil was unable to adapt its coffee policies toward world conditions, the reason was not foreign politics but domestic politics. "Political underdevelopment, not imperialism, was the principal constraint on Brazilian coffee policy."

_____. "Oil is the Exception." FOREIGN POLICY 14 (Spring 1974): 68-83.

Argues that Third World countries holding important primary commodities will be unable to establish effective cartels against the United States. Oil is the exception.

Kravis, Irving B. "International Commodity Agreements to Promote Aid and Efficiency: The Case of Coffee." CANADIAN JOURNAL OF ECONOMICS 1 (March 1960): 13-35.

Mason, Edward [S.]. CONTROLLING WORLD TRADE: CARTELS AND COMMODITY AGREEMENTS. New York: McGraw-Hill Book Co., 1946. 289 p.

Although commodity agreements may be desirable at times, cartels are never justified as they promote the economic interests of a small group of nations rather than of the public in general.

Mikdashi, Zuhayr. "Collusion Could Work." FOREIGN POLICY 14 (Spring 1974): 57-67.

LDCs with important raw materials may be able to develop cooperative policies to raise their commodity prices. Whether they will be successful or not depends on various economic and political factors, some of which are discussed by the writer.

_____. "Cooperation Among Oil Exporting Countries with Special Reference to Arab Countries: A Political Economy Analysis." INTERNATIONAL ORGANIZATION 28 (Winter 1974): 1-30.

Price, David E. "The Politics of Sugar." REVIEW OF POLITICS 33 (April 1971): 212-32.

A study of the domestic politics of making laws governing sugar quotas.

Rowe, J.W.F. PRIMARY COMMODITIES IN INTERNATIONAL TRADE. Cambridge: At the University Press, 1965. xi, 224 p.

Examines the role and impact of primary product commodity agreements. Part 4 of the study provides a valuable historical overview of the use and effectiveness of commodity agreements in the twentieth century.

Smith, Ian. "Sugar Markets in Disarray." JOURNAL OF WORLD TRADE LAW 9 (January-February 1975): 41-62.

A discussion of the international politics of the international sugar market in the light of imminent structural changes by the European Community and the United States.

Stocking, George W., and Watkins, Myron W. CARTELS IN ACTION. New York: Twentieth Century Fund, 1946. 533 p.

Case studies of selected twentieth-century cartels.

Wasserman, Ursula. "The International Cocoa Agreement." JOURNAL OF WORLD TRADE LAW 7 (January-February 1973): 129-34.

A discussion of the international cocoa agreement of October, 1972.

C. ECONOMIC SANCTIONS

Adler-Karlsson, Gunnar. "International Economic Power: The U.S. Strategic Embargo." JOURNAL OF WORLD TRADE LAW 6 (September-October 1972): 501-17.

A discussion of the nature and effectiveness of the U.S. strategic embargo against the Communist-bloc states.

Baer, George W. "Sanctions and Security: The League of Nations and the Italian-Ethiopian War, 1935-1936." INTERNATIONAL ORGANIZATION 27 (Spring 1973): 165-80.

Baldwin, David [A.]. "The Power of Positive Sanctions." WORLD POLITICS 24 (October 1971): 19-38.

An analysis of the differences between negative and positive sanctions.

Brown-John, C. Lloyd. MULTILATERAL SANCTIONS IN INTERNATIONAL LAW. New York: Praeger Publishers, 1975. 448 p.

Examines empirically the effectiveness of economic sanctions as a tool of international law enforcement and finds that they can be useful, particularly when used in connection with significant political pressures. The analysis focuses on sanctions toward Italy, the Dominican Republic, and Rhodesia.

Curtin, Timothy R.C., and Murray, David. ECONOMIC SANCTIONS AND RHODESIA; AN EXAMINATION OF THE PROBABLE EFFECT OF SANCTIONS ON NATIONAL AND PERSONAL INCOMES IN RHODESIA AND OF THE EFFECTIVENESS OF SANCTIONS ON RHODESIAN POLICY. London: Institute of Economic Affairs, 1967. 56 p.

Delaisi, Francis. "The Fallacy of Economic Sanctions." NEW COMMONWEALTH 2 (November 1934): 208-9.

Doxey, Margaret P. ECONOMIC SANCTIONS AND INTERNATIONAL ENFORCEMENT. Published for the Royal Institute of International Affairs. London: Oxford University Press, 1971. 162 p.

A short, informative study of economic sanctions of regional and international organizations. The volume is essential reading for anyone interested in the subject.

_____. "International Sanctions: A Framework for Analysis with Special Reference to the U.N. and Southern Africa." INTERNATIONAL ORGANIZA-TION 26 (Summer 1972): 527-50.

The author presents an analytical framework on international sanc-tions and then uses it to discuss some of the principal problems of U.N. sanctions toward Rhodesia and South Africa.

_____. "The Rhodesian Sanctions Experiment." YEAR BOOK OF WORLD AFFAIRS 25 (1971): 142-62.

Doxey examines the nature, implementation, and effectiveness of economic sanctions on Rhodesia.

Francis, E.V. "The Blockade and the New Economic Order." POLITICAL QUARTERLY 12 (1941): 40-52.

Galtung, Johan. "On the Effects of International Economic Sanctions with Examples from the Case of Rhodesia." WORLD POLITICS 19 (April 1967): 378-416.

Grieve, Muriel J. "Economic Sanctions: Theory and Practice." INTERNA-TIONAL RELATIONS 3 (October 1968): 431-43.

Hoffman, Fredrik. "The Function of Economic Sanctions: A Comparative Analysis." JOURNAL OF PEACE RESEARCH 4 (1967): 140-59.

A comparative analysis of the use of economic sanctions by the League of Nations against Italy in 1935 and by Great Britain against Rhodesia in 1965. Hoffman suggests that the League's application of sanctions was based largely on outdated, legalistic theories, while the British policy toward Rhodesia was largely an "escape" from political cross-pressures. In general, Hoffman be-lieves there is a low probability that economic sanctions will be successful.

Hyde, C.C., and Wehle, Louis B. "The Boycott in Foreign Affairs." AMERI-CAN JOURNAL OF INTERNATIONAL LAW 27 (1933): 1-10.

A discussion of some of the problems of implementing economic boycotts.

MacDonald, R. St. J. "Economic Sanctions in the International System." CANADIAN YEARBOOK OF INTERNATIONAL LAW 7 (1969): 61-91.

McKinnell, Robert T. "Sanctions and the Rhodesian Economy." JOURNAL OF MODERN AFRICAN STUDIES 7 (1969): 559-81.

Medlicott, William N. THE ECONOMIC BLOCKADE. London: His Majesty's Stationery Office, 1952. 732 p.

> A thorough and painstaking historical study of Great Britain's Second World War economic warfare against Germany, Italy, and Japan.

Mudge, G.A. "Domestic Policies and U.N. Activities: The Cases of Rhodesia and the Republic of South Africa." INTERNATIONAL ORGANIZATION 21 (Winter 1967): 55-78.

> Examines the political impact that U.N. policies have on the domestic politics of Rhodesia and the Republic of South Africa. Mudge suggests that political pressure from the United Nations has tended to politicize the issue of apartheid in both states.

Muir, J. Dapray. "The Boycott in International Law." JOURNAL OF INTERNATIONAL LAW AND ECONOMICS 9 (August 1974): 187-204.

> Examines the legality of the boycott under international law and finds that "about all that can be said at present with respect to the status of the boycott under international law is that a number of countries and commentators have suggested that it ought to be prohibited by law."

Segal, R., ed. SANCTIONS AGAINST SOUTH AFRICA. Harmondsworth, Engl.: Penguin Books, 1964. 272 p.

> A series of articles prepared for the 1964 London International Conference on Economic Sanctions against South Africa.

Spulber, Nicolas. "Effects of the Embargo on Soviet Trade." HARVARD BUSINESS REVIEW 30 (November-December 1952): 122-28.

> Finds that the U.S. embargo on the Soviet Union has been partially successful since the amount of Soviet trade has been kept below prewar levels. According to Spulber the major impact of the embargo has been not so much the control of the level of trade as the increase in the prices of goods.

Strange, Susan. "The Strategic Trade Embargoes: Sense or Nonsense?" YEAR BOOK OF WORLD AFFAIRS 12 (1958): 55-73.

> Strange analyzes the nature and effectiveness of the Anglo-American economic sanctions toward Communist states and concludes that such pressures should be dropped. Embargoes are ineffective and sometimes even counterproductive.

Sutcliffe, R.B. "The Political Economy of Rhodesian Sanctions." JOURNAL OF COMMONWEALTH POLITICAL STUDIES 7 (July 1969): 113-25.

Taubenfield, Howard J., and Taubenfield, Rita F. "The 'Economic Weapon': The League and the United Nations." PROCEEDINGS OF THE AMERICAN SOCIETY OF INTERNATIONAL LAW 58 (1964): 183-205.

> Based on a review of the League's and United Nations' use of economic sanctions, the authors conclude that such measures are a weak and crude political instrument. Furthermore, economic pressures have tended to unify opinion within the sanctioned area and to undermine the unity of the world community. Sanctions should be used only when there is a clear violation of international law and where the sanctions have a chance for success.

Wallensteen, Peter. "Characteristics of Economic Sanctions." JOURNAL OF PEACE RESEARCH 5 (1968): 248-67.

> A review of ten cases where economic sanctions were applied. Wallensteen suggests that sanctions have been somewhat effective in protecting or condemning a particular situation but that they have not been an effective influence on the behavior of a nation.

Wilczynski, J[oseph]. "Strategic Embargo in Perspective." SOVIET STUDIES 19 (1967): 74-86.

Zacklin, Ralph. "Challenge of Rhodesia: Toward an International Public Policy." INTERNATIONAL CONCILIATION, no. 575 (November 1969): 1-72.

> An analysis of the nature, justification, and implementation of U.N. economic sanctions on Rhodesia.

Chapter 4
THE POLITICS AND ECONOMICS
OF REGIONAL INTEGRATION

Regional integration is the process by which the traditional boundaries of nation states are broken down as states become more interdependent economically, socially, and politically. The phenomenon of regional integration has become particularly important in the contemporary international system because of the successful European experiment in integration, an experiment that has resulted in significant economic gains to its member states. As a result, other regions of the world, particularly Latin America and Africa, have attempted to forge regional common markets in an attempt to duplicate the European regional system.

Although regional integration has been viewed largely as an economic phenomenon, politics plays an important role in the creation and maintenance of common markets and in the broader movements of regional integration. Since states seek to maximize their national interests, they will join integration organizations only when it is in their national interest to do so. Once regional structures are created, however, the new transnational forces themselves exert political influence on both member and nonmember states. This means that movements of regional integration themselves become important political forces which influence the international system and more particularly the foreign policies of individual states. In this chapter some of the important information sources on the political economy of regional integration are examined. The first part of the literature focuses on theoretical and methodological studies; the second and third parts discuss studies on the integration experiences of Europe and of other areas.

A. THEORIES AND METHODS OF INTEGRATION

Balassa, Bela. THE THEORY OF ECONOMIC INTEGRATION. Homewood, Ill.: Richard D. Irwin, 1961. xiii, 304 p.

A standard theoretical study of the process of economic integration.

Caporaso, James A. "Theory and Method in the Study of International Integration." INTERNATIONAL ORGANIZATION 25 (Spring 1971): 228-53.

Claude, Inis L., Jr. SWORDS INTO PLOWSHARES; THE PROBLEMS AND PROGRESS OF INTERNATIONAL ORGANIZATION. 4th ed. New York: Random House, 1971. xii, 514 p.

Chapter 17 of this international organization text provides an excellent critical analysis of the functional approach to peace.

Etzioni, Amitai. POLITICAL UNIFICATION: A COMPARATIVE STUDY OF LEADERS AND FORCES. New York: Holt, Rinehart and Winston, 1965. 346 p.

A sociological framework of integration is developed and then applied to the European integration movement.

Fisher, William E. "An Analysis of the Deutsch Sociocausal Paradigm of Political Integration." INTERNATIONAL ORGANIZATION 23 (Spring 1969): 254-90.

Friedrich, Carl J. TRENDS OF FEDERALISM IN THEORY AND PRACTICE. New York: Praeger Publishers, 1968. xii, 193 p.

Haas, Ernst B. BEYOND THE NATION-STATE; FUNCTIONALISM AND INTERNATIONAL ORGANIZATION. Stanford, Calif.: Stanford University Press, 1964. 595 p.

Building on functionalism and systems theory, Haas develops a theory of integration involving both governmental and nongovernmental economic and social transactions. Transactions will not themselves lead to integration but must be accompanied by political action of international organizations. A pioneering study.

_____. "International Integration: The European and Universal Process." INTERNATIONAL ORGANIZATION 15 (Summer 1961): 366-92.

_____. "Regionalism, Functionalism, and Universal International Organization." WORLD POLITICS 8 (January 1956): 238-63.

Haas, Ernst B., and Schmitter, Philippe C. "Economics and Differential Patterns of Political Integration: Projections about Unity in Latin America." INTERNATIONAL ORGANIZATION 18 (July 1964): 705-37.

Hansen, Roger D. "Regional Integration: Reflections on a Decade of Theoretical Efforts." WORLD POLITICS 21 (January 1969): 242-71.

An overview of the theory and practice of regional integration of the 1960s. The study focuses on the performance of the integration movements in Europe, East Africa, and Central America.

Hoffman, Stanley. "Obstinate or Obsolete? The Fate of the Nation-State and the Case of Western Europe." DAEDALUS 95 (Summer 1966): 862-915.

Hoffman argues for the "logic of diversity" as it is contrasted with Haas's "logic of integration."

Kaiser, Karl. "Transactional Politics: Toward a Theory of Multinational Politics." INTERNATIONAL ORGANIZATION 25 (Autumn 1971): 790-817.

Krauss, Melvyn B., ed. THE ECONOMICS OF INTEGRATION. London: George Allen & Unwin, 1973. 300 p.

A collection of readings on different facets of economic integration, including the theories of customs union, monetary union, and tax harmonization.

Lindberg, Leon N., and Scheingold, Stuart A., eds. REGIONAL INTEGRATION: THEORY AND RESEARCH. Cambridge, Mass.: Harvard University Press, 1971. 398 p.

These articles, originally published in the Autumn 1970 issue of INTERNATIONAL ORGANIZATION, grew out of a conference on regional integration at the University of Wisconsin. The essays examine and evaluate the major developments in the theory of integration and offer some new avenues of empirical investigation.

Lipsey, Richard G. "The Theory of Customs Unions: A General Survey." ECONOMIC JOURNAL 70 (September 1960): 496-513.

A survey of major developments in the theory of customs unions.

Mitrany, David. "The Functional Approach in Historical Perspective." INTERNATIONAL AFFAIRS 47 (July 1971): 532-43.

_____. "The Functional Approach to World Organization." INTERNATIONAL AFFAIRS 29 (July 1948): 350-63.

Compares the functional and political-constitutional approaches to peace and suggests that the development of the world stands at a "crossroad" in its search for a new world order.

_____. A WORKING PEACE SYSTEM: AN ARGUMENT FOR THE FUNCTIONAL DEVELOPMENT OF INTERNATIONAL ORGANIZATION. Oxford: Oxford University Press, 1944. 60 p.

Mitrany, the father of "functionalism," sets forth the basic theory of the functional approach to peace. Peace will be achieved, according to him, not by eliminating nation-states but by encouraging functional cooperation among them. The outcome of increased cooperation will be the creation of a broad international community of men and women.

Morse, Edward L. "The Politics of Interdependence." INTERNATIONAL OR-
GANIZATION 23 (Spring 1969): 311-26.

   A critical analysis of regional integration studies of the late 1960s.

Nye, Joseph S., Jr. PEACE IN PARTS: INTEGRATION AND CONFLICT
IN REGIONAL ORGANIZATION. Boston: Little, Brown and Co., 1971.
199 p.

   Nye reviews hypotheses on the relationship between peace and regionalism, discusses the various dimensions of the concept of regional integration, and offers a political model of economic integration. One of the most helpful parts of the study is chapter 4,
   "Economic Integration and Conflict Resolution," in which the author suggests that regional integration can serve as an instrument
   of peacekeeping.

Puchala, Donald J. "International Transactions and Regional Integration."
INTERNATIONAL ORGANIZATION 24 (Autumn 1970): 732-63.

   Explores the values and limitations of transactional analysis.

Robson, Peter. INTERNATIONAL ECONOMIC INTEGRATION; SELECTED
READINGS. Harmondsworth, Engl.: Penguin Books, 1972. 458 p.

   Essays on different aspects of the theory of economic integration.

Russett, Bruce. "Transactions, Community, and International Political Integration." JOURNAL OF COMMON MARKET STUDIES 9 (March 1971): 224-48.

   A theoretical discussion of the relationship of transactions flows to
   political integration.

Sewell, James Patrick. FUNCTIONALISM AND WORLD POLITICS. Princeton, N.J.: Princeton University Press, 1966. 332 p.

   Probably the most significant attempt to verify empirically the
   functionalist theory of international relations. Sewell tests the
   theory by examining the U.N. programs financing economic development, and finds that the functionalist thesis does not explain
   the behavior of U.N. economic programs. Technical self-determi-
   nation does not fully explain how or why the programs developed
   the way they did. A helpful bibliography is appended.

Tollison, Robert D., and Willett, Thomas D. "International Integration and
the Interdependence of Economic Variables." INTERNATIONAL ORGANIZA-
TION 27 (Spring 1973): 255-71.

   A discussion of the concepts of integration and interdependence
   and how they might be measured quantitatively.

Viner, Jacob. THE CUSTOMS UNION ISSUE. New York: Carnegie Endowment for International Peace, 1950. viii, 221 p.

> A classic study of the economic gains and losses from the establishment of a customs union.

B. REGIONAL INTEGRATION: EUROPE

Alting Von Geusau, Frans A.M. BEYOND THE EUROPEAN COMMUNITY. Leiden, Netherlands: A.W. Sijthoff, 1969. 247 p.

> Examines the major economic and institutional developments in the European Community. An attempt is made to explain why economic integration has not resulted in political integration.

Bailey, Richard. THE EUROPEAN COMMUNITY IN THE WORLD. London: Hutchinson and Co., 1973. 200 p.

> A study of the international economic relations of the European Community with nonmember European states, former African colonies, the Third World, members of the British Commonwealth, the United States, and the European Socialist states (COMECON).

Brenner, Michael J. TECHNOCRATIC POLITICS AND THE FUNCTIONALIST THEORY OF EUROPEAN INTEGRATION. Cornell Research Papers in International Studies, no. 7. Ithaca, N.Y.: Cornell University Press, 1969. 164 p.

Camps, Miriam. EUROPEAN UNIFICATION IN THE SIXTIES; FROM VETO TO THE CRISIS. Published for the Council on Foreign Relations. New York: McGraw-Hill Book Co., 1966. xii, 273 p.

> An analytic historical account of the political tensions and dynamics of the EEC during the first half of the 1960s. The study focuses on the French veto of Britain's entry into the Community and on the crisis on agricultural policy.

Clark, William H. THE POLITICS OF THE COMMON MARKET. Englewood Cliffs, N.J.: Prentice-Hall, 1967. xi, 180 p.

Coombes, David. POLITICS AND BUREAUCRACY IN THE EUROPEAN COMMUNITY; A PORTRAIT OF THE COMMISSION OF THE E.E.C. London: George Allen & Unwin, 1970. 343 p.

> A straightforward account of the structure, function, and performance of the EEC Commission in terms of its promotion of the integration movement.

Curzon, Gerard, and Curzon, Victoria. "Neo-Colonialism and the European Economic Community." YEAR BOOK OF WORLD AFFAIRS 25 (1971): 118-41.

A review and appraisal of the economic relations between the
European Community and African states. The authors suggest that
the trade relations worked out through the Yaounde Convention
are not themselves neocolonial or neoimperialistic.

Dahrendorf, Ralf. "Possibilities and Limits of a European Community Foreign
Policy." In THE EUROPEAN COMMUNITY IN THE 1970'S, edited by Steven
J. Warnecke, pp. 111-26. New York: Praeger Publishers, 1972.

Examines some of the difficulties in establishing common commercial policies in order to develop a more realistic view as to the
possibilities of a common foreign policy.

Diebold, William, Jr. "The Economic Issues Between the European Community
and the United States in the 1970's: An American Perspective." In THE EURO-
PEAN COMMUNITY IN THE 1970'S, edited by Steven J. Warnecke, pp. 89-
110. New York: Praeger Publishers, 1972.

Feld, Werner J. "Political Aspects of Transnational Business Collaboration in
the Common Market." INTERNATIONAL ORGANIZATION 24 (Spring 1970):
209-38.

Investigates the impact of the MNC on the European Community.
Discussion is based on fifty in-depth interviews with business executives and governmental officials.

_____. TRANSNATIONAL BUSINESS COLLABORATION AMONG COMMON
MARKET COUNTRIES: ITS IMPLICATION FOR POLITICAL INTEGRATION.
New York: Praeger Publishers, 1970. 137 p.

Using a neofunctional framework, the author examines the possible
impact of MNCs on the Common Market and finds that while the
political effects have been limited there have been many beneficial economic results.

Friedrich, Carl J. EUROPE: AN EMERGENT NATION? New York: Harper
& Row, 1969. 269 p.

A general empirical investigation of the socialization and informal
community building processes operating in the European Community.

Galtung, Johan. THE EUROPEAN COMMUNITY: A SUPERPOWER IN THE
MAKING. London: George Allen & Unwin, 1973. 194 p.

Galtung deplores the rise of the EEC's superpower status and particularly its commercial relations with the Third World. Some suggestions are offered on how the community might foster world economic
equity.

Haas, Ernst B. THE UNITING OF EUROPE: POLITICAL, SOCIAL AND ECO-

NOMIC FORCES, 1950-1957. Stanford, Calif.: Stanford University Press, 1958. 552 p.

One of the early important analytical studies of the European integration movement.

Hallstein, Walter. UNITED EUROPE, CHALLENGE AND OPPORTUNITY. Cambridge, Mass.: Harvard University Press, 1962. 109 p.

Hallstein, one of the early leaders of the European integration movement, discusses the historical, economic, and political dimensions of Europe's integration experiment. The material in this short, readable book was originally delivered as the William Clayton Lectures at the Fletcher School of Law and Diplomacy.

Hansen, Roger D. "European Integration: Forward March, Parade Rest, or Dismissed?" INTERNATIONAL ORGANIZATION 27 (Spring 1973): 225-54.

A careful critical analysis of Leon N. Lindberg and Stuart A. Scheingold's two books on European integration, EUROPE'S WOULD-BE POLITY and REGIONAL INTEGRATION: THEORY AND RESEARCH.

Hinshaw, Randall. THE EUROPEAN COMMUNITY AND AMERICAN TRADE; A STUDY IN ATLANTIC ECONOMICS AND POLICY. Published for the Council on Foreign Relations. New York: Praeger Publishers, 1965. 188 p.

Examines economic changes brought about by the Common Market in order to draw trade policy implications for the United States.

Hirsch, Fred. "The Political Economics of European Monetary Integration." WORLD TODAY 28 (October 1972): 424-33.

The long-range movement toward European monetary integration impedes the immediate need for flexible exchange rates. Given the difficulties of establishing a common currency, Hirsch argues that a new strategy should be developed which would encourage monetary union but which would also meet the present needs of regional finance.

Inglehart, Ronald. "An End to European Integration?" AMERICAN POLITICAL SCIENCE REVIEW 61 (March 1967): 91-105.

Ionescu, Ghita, comp. THE NEW POLITICS OF EUROPEAN INTEGRATION. New York: St. Martin's Press, 1972. xv, 278 p.

A collection of studies on the political structures and dynamics of the EEC. The articles appeared earlier in the comparative politics journal GOVERNMENT AND OPPOSITION.

Kerr, H.H., Jr. "Changing Attitudes Through International Participation:

European Parliaments and Integration." INTERNATIONAL ORGANIZATION 27 (Winter 1973): 45-84.

Kitzinger, Uwe. DIPLOMACY AND PERSUASION: HOW BRITAIN JOINED THE COMMON MARKET. London: Thames and Hudson, 1973. 432 p.

> A comprehensive account of British domestic politics resulting from the government's decision to join the European Community.

_____. THE POLITICS AND ECONOMICS OF EUROPEAN INTEGRATION; BRITAIN, EUROPE, AND THE UNITED STATES. New York: Praeger Publishers, 1963. 246 p.

> A valuable but dated discussion of the political basis of the EEC.

_____. "Problems of a European Political Economy." In THE EUROPEAN COMMUNITY IN THE 1970'S, edited by Steven J. Warnecke, pp. 29-52. New York: Praeger Publishers, 1972.

> Sketches some of the important domestic and international economic issues facing the European Community and discusses the institutional requirements for dealing with them.

Kohnstamm, Max, and Hager, Wolfgang, eds. A NATION WRIT LARGE? FOREIGN POLICY PROBLEMS BEFORE THE EUROPEAN COMMUNITY. New York: John Wiley & Sons, 1973. 275 p.

> These essays examine various foreign political and economic issues facing the European Community, among them trade, monetary reform, East-West relations, relations with the LDCs, and European security.

Krause, Lawrence B. EUROPEAN ECONOMIC INTEGRATION AND THE UNITED STATES. Washington, D.C.: Brookings Institution, 1968. 265 p.

> Examines the policies and programs of the EEC and the EFTA during the 1960s and then sets forth policy implications for United States' relations with Western Europe.

Lindberg, Leon N. THE POLITICAL DYNAMICS OF EUROPEAN ECONOMIC INTEGRATION. Stanford, Calif.: Stanford University Press, 1963. 367 p.

> An analysis of the political institutions and policy-making process of the EEC. The dynamics of the EEC institutions are examined through four case studies.

Lindberg, Leon N., and Scheingold, Stuart A. EUROPE'S WOULD-BE POLITY; PATTERNS OF CHANGE IN THE EUROPEAN COMMUNITY. Englewood Cliffs, N.J.: Prentice-Hall, 1970. vi, 314 p.

> A sophisticated analysis of the accomplishments and institutional

developments of the EEC with a view of developing a model to project and guide the future of the Community.

Mahotiere, Stuart R. de la. TOWARDS ONE EUROPE. Harmondsworth, Engl.: Penguin Books, 1970. 332 p.

A useful introduction to the politics and economics of the European integration movement.

Mally, Gerhard. THE EUROPEAN COMMUNITY IN PERSPECTIVE; THE NEW EUROPE, THE UNITED STATES, AND THE WORLD. Lexington, Mass.: Lexington Books, 1973. xxvi, 349 p.

An up-to-date analysis of European integration, focusing on concepts and theories, the internal dynamics of the European Community, and the future of the integration movement. Chapter 7 on alternative political structures for the European region is illuminating.

Malmgren, Harald B. "Europe, the United States, and the World Economy." In THE EUROPEAN COMMUNITY IN THE 1970'S, edited by Steven J. Warnecke, pp. 127-48. New York: Praeger Publishers, 1972.

Reviews the changing dimensions of U.S.-European political and economic relations.

Neunreither, Karlheinz. "Transformation of a Political Role: Reconsidering the Case of the Commission of the European Communities." JOURNAL OF COMMON MARKET STUDIES 10 (March 1972): 233-48.

Niblock, Michael. THE E.E.C.: NATIONAL PARLIAMENTS IN COMMUNITY DECISION MAKING. London: Chatham House, 1971. 111 p.

Investigates the relationship of the EEC Parliament to the national parliaments of the community's member states. An attempt is made to assess the impact of the former on the latter and vice-versa.

Pinder, John. "Positive Integration and Negative Integration: Some Problems of Economic Union in the E.E.C." WORLD TODAY 24 (March 1968): 88-110.

The first part of this article reviews the literature on economic integration; the second part examines the European integration experience and some of its difficulties.

Sommer, Theo. "The Community is Working." FOREIGN AFFAIRS 51 (July 1973): 747-60.

Despite numerous setbacks, the European Community is working and is on its way to further growth and development.

Spinelli, Altiero. THE EUROCRATS; CONFLICT AND CRISIS IN THE EURO-
PEAN COMMUNITY. Baltimore: Johns Hopkins University Press, 1967. 229 p.

Swann, Dennis. THE ECONOMICS OF THE COMMON MARKET. 2d ed.
Harmondsworth, Engl.: Penguin Books, 1972. 223 p.

> A nontechnical account of the economic programs and policies of
> the EEC. The study examines commercial policy, factor move-
> ments, regional and social policy, and foreign relations. Particu-
> larly useful is chapter 5, which reviews the common policies in
> agriculture, transportation, and energy.

Warnecke, Steven J., ed. THE EUROPEAN COMMUNITY IN THE 1970'S.
New York: Praeger Publishers, 1972. xviii, 228 p.

> A collection of eleven essays on aspects of the European Commu-
> nity's future development. Some of the essays are noted elsewhere
> in this chapter.

C. REGIONAL INTEGRATION:
AFRICA, ASIA, AND LATIN AMERICA

Adams, Gordon. "Community Foreign Policy and Political Integration: Lessons
of the African Association." In THE EUROPEAN COMMUNITY IN THE 1970'S,
edited by Steven J. Warnecke, pp. 207-19. New York: Praeger Publishers,
1972.

> Adams examines the attempt by the European Community to develop
> a common foreign policy toward the Associated African and Mala-
> gasy States (AAMS) and finds that national and not common inter-
> ests are the chief determinants of policies. Regional integration
> is more "a figment of the theorists' imagination than a reality."

Avery, William P., and Cochrane, James D. "Innovation in Latin American
Regionalism: The Andean Common Market." INTERNATIONAL ORGANIZA-
TION 27 (Spring 1973): 181-224.

Bentil, J. Kodwo. "The Legal Framework and the Economic Aspects of the
East African Common Market." JOURNAL OF LAW AND ECONOMIC DE-
VELOPMENT 4 (Spring 1969): 27-47.

Brester, Havelock, and Thomas, Clive Y. THE DYNAMICS OF WEST INDIAN
ECONOMIC INTEGRATION. Studies in Regional Economic Integration, vol. 1.
Jamaica: Institute of Social and Economic Research, University of the West
Indies, 1967. xx, 335 p.

Cochrane, James D., and Cloan, John W. "LAFTA and the CACM: A Comparative Analysis of Integration in Latin America." JOURNAL OF DEVELOP-
ING AREAS 8 (October 1973): 13-38.

A comparative analysis of the major factors encouraging and impeding the process of economic integration in the Latin American Free Trade Association and the Central American Common Market.

Curzon, Victoria. THE ESSENTIALS OF ECONOMIC INTEGRATION: LESSONS OF E.F.T.A. EXPERIENCE. New York: St. Martin's Press, 1974. xii, 319 p.

Based on a case study of the European Free Trade Association, this study suggests that free trade associations may be more efficient than customs unions in promoting economic integration when the member countries' tariff structures are not greatly different.

Dell, Sidney. A LATIN AMERICAN COMMON MARKET? London: Oxford University Press, 1966. 336 p.

A study of the political and economic dynamics of the Latin American Free Trade Association.

_____. TRADE BLOCKS AND COMMON MARKETS. New York: Alfred A. Knopf, 1963. 384 p.

A general overview of the impact of the European integration experiment on global trading patterns.

Diab, Muhammad A. "The Arab Common Market." JOURNAL OF COMMON MARKET STUDIES 4 (May 1966): 238-50.

Griffin, Keith [B.], and Ffrench-Davis, Ricardo. "Customs Unions and Latin American Integration." JOURNAL OF COMMON MARKET STUDIES 4 (October 1965): 1-21.

Grunwald, Joseph; Wionczek, Miguel S.; and Carnoy, Martin. LATIN AMERICAN ECONOMIC INTEGRATION AND U.S. POLICY. Washington, D.C.: Brookings Institution, 1972. 210 p.

An examination of Latin American economic integration and the U.S. policies toward it. The policy analysis focuses on aid, private foreign investment, and trade.

Haas, Ernst B., and Schmitter, Philippe C. "Economics and Differential Patterns of Political Integration: Projections about Unity in Latin America." INTERNATIONAL ORGANIZATION 18 (Autumn 1964): 705-37.

_____. THE POLITICS OF ECONOMICS IN LATIN AMERICAN REGIONALISM: THE LATIN AMERICAN FREE TRADE ASSOCIATION AFTER FOUR YEARS OF OPERATION. Denver, Colo.: University of Denver Social Science Foundation and Graduate School of International Studies, 1965. 78 p.

An excellent theoretical study of the political processes involved in the development of LAFTA.

Hazlewood, Arthur, ed. AFRICAN INTEGRATION AND DISINTEGRATION; CASE STUDIES IN ECONOMIC AND POLITICAL UNION. London: Oxford University Press, 1967. 414 p.

Of the ten essays on African integration, the first four examine selected attempts at regional economic integration and the remaining six focus on the political unity within individual states.

Karefa-Smart, John, ed. AFRICA: PROGRESS THROUGH COOPERATION. New York: Dodd, Mead & Co., 1966. xvi, 288 p.

Kaser, Michael. COMECON: INTEGRATION PROBLEMS OF THE PLANNED ECONOMIES. London: Oxford University Press, 1965. vi, 215 p.

A study of the role of COMECON, the Soviet-bloc trade organization concerned with increasing economic integration of Socialist economies. The study examines the history of the organization as well as policy problems that have impeded the integration process.

Krause, Walter, and Mathis, F. John. LATIN AMERICA AND ECONOMIC INTEGRATION: REGIONAL PLANNING AND DEVELOPMENT. Iowa City: University of Iowa Press, 1970. 104 p.

A short, lucid account of the Latin American program for economic integration as a means of stimulating regional economic development.

Milensky, Edward S. THE POLITICS OF REGIONAL ORGANIZATION IN LATIN AMERICA: THE LATIN AMERICAN FREE TRADE ASSOCIATION. New York: Praeger Publishers, 1973. 289 p.

A study of the political dynamics of LAFTA from 1960 through 1972. Chapter 5 on "The Politics of Trade" presents a careful analysis of the problems involved in negotiating common commercial policies.

Morawetz, David. THE ANDEAN GROUP: A CASE STUDY IN ECONOMIC INTEGRATION AMONG DEVELOPING COUNTRIES. Cambridge, Mass.: M.I.T. Press, 1974. x, 171 p.

Examines the economic integration movement among Bolivia, Chile, Colombia, Ecuador, Peru, and Venezuela.

Navarrete, Jorge E. "Latin American Economic Integration--A Survey of Recent Literature." JOURNAL OF COMMON MARKET STUDIES 4 (December 1965): 168-77.

A bibliographical essay based on sixty-six books and articles on Latin American integration.

Ndegwa, Philip. THE COMMON MARKET AND DEVELOPMENT IN EAST AFRICA. 2d ed. Nairobi, Kenya: East African Publishing House, 1968. 228 p.

An economic study of the structure, dynamics, and effects of trade among three East African Common Market States (Kenya, Uganda, and Tanganyika) as well as with other nonmember states.

Orantes, Isaac Cohen. REGIONAL INTEGRATION IN CENTRAL AMERICA. Lexington, Mass.: Lexington Books, 1972. 126 p.

Describes the origins, processes, and difficulties of the Central American Common Market. Particularly useful are chapters 2 and 3 which discuss the influence on the integration movement of the U.N. Economic Commission for Latin America (ECLA) and the United States.

Robson, Peter. ECONOMIC INTEGRATION IN AFRICA. Evanston, Ill.: Northwestern University Press, 1968. 320 p.

Segal, Aaron. THE POLITICS OF CARIBBEAN ECONOMIC INTEGRATION. Puerto Rico: Institute of Caribbean Studies, University of Puerto Rico, 1968. 156 p.

Despite its title, this study is primarily an economic analysis of the integration movement among Caribbean nations.

Schmitter, Philippe C., and Haas, Ernst B. MEXICO AND LATIN AMERICAN ECONOMIC INTEGRATION. Research Series, no. 5. Berkeley: Institute of International Studies, University of California, 1964. 43 p.

Stonham, P.E. "Intra-Regional Trade Co-operation in Developing Asia." JOURNAL OF COMMON MARKET STUDIES 6 (December 1967): 197-210.

Wilkinson, Joe R. LATIN AMERICA AND THE EUROPEAN ECONOMIC COMMUNITY: AN APPRAISAL. Monograph Series in World Affairs, no. 4. Denver, Colo.: Social Science Foundation and Graduate School of International Studies, University of Denver, 1964. 65 p.

Wionczek, Miguel S. "The Present Status of Latin American Integration Attempts." In CONTINUING ISSUES IN INTERNATIONAL POLITICS, edited by Yale Ferguson and Walter Weiker, pp. 383-401. Pacific Palisades, Calif.: Goodyear Publishing Co., 1973.

Explains why the Latin American Free Trade Association and the

Central American Common Market have had such limited success in bringing about economic and political union. The author is skeptical of the establishment of a Latin American common market by 1985.

_____. "The Rise and Decline of Latin American Economic Integration." JOURNAL OF COMMON MARKET STUDIES 9 (September 1970): 49-66.

A study of the rise and fall of the CACM and LAFTA.

_____, ed. ECONOMIC COOPERATION IN LATIN AMERICA, AFRICA, AND ASIA. Cambridge, Mass.: M.I.T. Press, 1969. xi, 566 p.

_____. LATIN AMERICAN ECONOMIC INTEGRATION: EXPERIENCES AND PROSPECTS. Rev. ed. New York: Praeger Publishers, 1966. 310 p.

A collection of theoretical and empirical studies on the CACM and LAFTA.

Chapter 5

POLITICS AND THE INTERNATIONAL MONETARY SYSTEM

The international monetary system is the system that coordinates and regulates the transnational financial relations of states. This involves, among other things, the coordination of national monetary policies, maintenance of stable exchange rates, and the creation and regulation of international liquidity. Although the international monetary system is chiefly an economic enterprise, the management of international finance is essentially a political process. Politics is a part of the policy-making process at the IMF and the World Bank; political concerns also play a significant role in the development of domestic and international monetary policies of individual states. The studies listed below represent some of the most significant contemporary research on the political economy of the international monetary system.

Aliber, Robert Z. CHOICES FOR THE DOLLAR; COSTS AND BENEFITS OF POSSIBLE APPROACHES TO THE BALANCE OF PAYMENTS PROBLEM. Washington, D.C.: National Planning Association, 1969. v, 54 p.

Aubrey, Henry G. BEHIND THE VEIL OF INTERNATIONAL MONEY. Essays in International Finance, no. 71. Princeton, N.J.: International Finance Section, Department of Economics, Princeton University, January 1969. 32 p.

Attempts to explain the American international financial deficit of the 1960s using both economic and political perspectives. Aubrey suggests that the best "dollar diplomacy" is to cooperate with European states.

_____. THE DOLLAR IN WORLD AFFAIRS: AN ESSAY IN INTERNATIONAL POLICY. Published for the Council on Foreign Relations. New York: Harper & Row, 1964. xii, 295 p.

Examines the historical relationship of the dollar to the international monetary system.

_____. "The Political Economy of International Monetary Reform." SOCIAL RESEARCH 33 (Summer 1966): 218-54.

The most difficult problems of international monetary reform are

not technical and economic but political. Indeed, the neglect
of the political element has complicated the movement toward
reform. Aubrey sketches some of the principal political problems
in bringing about changes in the international monetary system.

Bergsten, C. Fred. "New Urgency for International Monetary Reform." FOR-
EIGN POLICY 19 (Summer 1975): 79-93.

Suggests that the continued use of gold and the dollar in the international monetary system poses serious problems to further development of the system. The best alternative is to vigorously
pursue a policy which makes SDRs the basis of the monetary system.

Boarman, Patrick M., and Tuerck, David G., eds. WORLD MONETARY DIS-
ORDER: NATIONAL POLICIES VERSUS INTERNATIONAL IMPERATIVES. New
York: Praeger Publishers, 1976. 200 p.

American and foreign international monetary authorities examine
some of the problems and prospects of establishing a new, more
effective international monetary system.

Bosman, Hans W.J., and Alting von Geusau, Frans A.M., eds. THE FU-
TURE OF THE INTERNATIONAL MONETARY SYSTEM. Leiden, Netherlands:
A.W. Sijthoff, 1970. 180 p.

The articles discuss the major international monetary system and problems of the 1960s, and offer some suggestions for creating a more
effective international monetary order.

Cleveland, Harold van Buren. "How the Dollar Standard Died." FOREIGN
POLICY 5 (Winter 1971-72): 41-51.

Cohen, Stephen D. INTERNATIONAL MONETARY REFORM, 1964-1969: THE
POLITICAL DIMENSION. New York: Praeger Publishers, 1970. 201 p.

The thesis of this pioneering study is that the international monetary reforms of the mid-1960s were ultimately based on political
interests of states.

Cooper, Richard N. "The Future of the Dollar." FOREIGN POLICY 11
(Summer 1973): 3-23.

"At the end of a decade the position of the dollar will not be
very different from what it is now. . . . The basic reason for this
simple forecast is simple: there is at present no clear, feasible
alternative."

_____. "Prolegomena to the Choice of an International Monetary System."
INTERNATIONAL ORGANIZATION 29 (Winter 1975): 63-98.

Discusses alternative international monetary regimes and then examines the major controversies over the establishment of a new system acceptable to all states. The major source of tension is not a conflict of interests but ignorance about the probable consequences of alternative monetary systems.

Gardner, Richard N. "The Politics of Liquidity." In THE POLITICS OF INTERNATIONAL ORGANIZATIONS, edited by Robert W. Cox, pp. 275-85. New York: Praeger Publishers, 1970.

A concise essay on the politics of creating SDRs within the International Monetary Fund. Gardner discusses some of the principal issues in the SDR negotiations and reviews some of the issues that will have to be dealt with in the future.

Grampp, William D. "International Politics and Dollar Policy." CHALLENGE, February 1965, pp. 20-23.

The major purpose of the international financial policy of the United States is political, not economic. It not only attempts to make the dollar a symbol of power but to create and maintain a financial network through which it can influence the decisions of other governments.

Hirsch, Fred. MONEY INTERNATIONAL: ECONOMICS AND POLITICS OF WORLD MONEY. Harmondsworth, Engl.: Penguin Books, 1969. 624 p.

A study of the operations, problems, and reform possibilities of the international monetary system. Despite its title, the focus of the study is primarily economic.

_____. AN SDR STANDARD: IMPETUS, ELEMENTS AND IMPEDIMENTS. Princeton Essays in International Finance, no. 99. Princeton, N.J.: International Finance Section, Department of Economics, Princeton University, June 1973. 29 p.

Johnson, Brian. THE POLITICS OF MONEY. New York: McGraw-Hill Book Co., 1970. xiv, 339 p.

Describes the international monetary system and some of its major problems in the late 1960s. The implication of this journalistic account is that political pressures have been a principal factor in the development and continuation of the system.

Johnson, Harry G. "Decline of the International Monetary System." WORLD TODAY 25 (March 1969): 103-9.

A brief study of some of the major weaknesses of the international monetary system.

Kenen, Peter B. "International Position of the Dollar in a Changing World. INTERNATIONAL ORGANIZATION 23 (Summer 1969): 705-18.

Kindleberger, Charles P. THE POLITICS OF MONEY AND WORLD LAN-
GUAGE. Princeton Essays in International Finance, no. 61. Princeton, N.J.:
International Finance Section, Department of Economics, Princeton University,
August 1967. 11 p.

> Argues that the dollar should be the foundation of the international
> monetary system not because of nationalistic or political considera-
> tions but because it can serve as the basis for an efficient system
> of international exchange. International considerations must be
> given greater emphasis than nationalistic concerns.

Krause, Lawrence B. "Private International Finance." In TRANSNATIONAL
RELATIONS AND WORLD POLITICS, edited by Robert O. Keohane and Joseph
S. Nye, Jr., pp. 173-90. Cambridge, Mass.: Harvard University Press, 1972.

> The increasing international flows of private capital have diminished
> monetary sovereignty of states. Krause suggests that the lack of
> effective control over a nation's monetary system is largely the re-
> sult of a failure to adapt to the changing international environment.

Machlup, Fritz. REMAKING THE INTERNATIONAL MONETARY SYSTEM; THE
RIO AGREEMENT AND BEYOND. Baltimore: Johns Hopkins Press, 1968.
161 p.

> An economic analysis of the meaning and significance of the 1967
> Rio Agreement which created SDRs.

McKinnon, Ronald I. PRIVATE AND OFFICIAL INTERNATIONAL MONEY:
THE CASE FOR THE DOLLAR. Princeton Essays in International Finance, no.
74. Princeton, N.J.: International Finance Section, Department of Economics,
Princeton University, April 1969. 40 p.

Mandel, Ernest. DECLINE OF THE DOLLAR: A MARXIST VIEW OF THE
MONETARY CRISIS. New York: Monad Press, n.d. Distributed by Path-
finder Press. 128 p.

> A collection of previously published essays on the international
> monetary system. The author, a Marxist, argues that the contem-
> porary international monetary system will eventually collapse be-
> cause of its inherent capitalistic contradictions.

Meier, Gerald M. PROBLEMS OF A WORLD MONETARY ORDER. New York:
Oxford University Press, 1974. xiii, 305 p.

> A study of three contemporary problems in the international eco-
> nomic system: international monetary crises, balance of payments
> tensions and the dollar, and the exchange-rate problem.

Mikesell, Raymond F., and Furth, J. Herbert. FOREIGN DOLLAR BALANCES
AND THE DOLLAR. New York: NBER, 1974. Distributed by Columbia University Press. xiv, 125 p.

The authors suggest that the dollar, despite its liquidity problems, will continue to play a dominant role in international financial transactions.

Monroe, Wilbur F. INTERNATIONAL MONETARY RECONSTRUCTION: PROBLEMS AND ISSUES. Lexington, Mass.: Lexington Books, 1974. 191 p.

A clear, balanced account of the issues and tensions of the international monetary system during the late 1960s and early 1970s. The focus is on the competing interests of the United States, Western Europe, and the developing nations.

Officer, Lawrence H., and Willett, Thomas D. THE INTERNATIONAL MONETARY SYSTEM; PROBLEMS AND PROPOSALS. Englewood Cliffs, N.J.: Prentice-Hall, 1969. xi, 238 p.

These essays analyze some of the causes of the international monetary problems of the last half of the 1960s and discuss the feasibility of alternative systems.

Oppenheimer, P.M. "Gold, the Dollar, and the World Economy." WORLD TODAY 24 (February 1968): 58-63.

Rolfe, Sidney E. GOLD AND WORLD POWER; THE DOLLAR, THE POUND, AND THE PLANS FOR REFORM. New York: Harper & Row, 1966. 276 p.

A discussion of the major shortcomings of the Bretton Woods system and the requirements for a new alternative system.

Roosa, Robert V. THE DOLLAR AND WORLD LIQUIDITY. New York: Random House, 1967. xiii, 367 p.

A collection of the author's articles and speeches on the role of the dollar in the international monetary system.

_____. MONETARY REFORM FOR THE WORLD ECONOMY. Published for the Council on Foreign Relations. New York: Harper & Row, 1965. 167 p.

Sets forth the requirements and policy recommendations for a desirable international monetary order.

Russell, Robert W. "Transgovernmental Interaction in the International Monetary System, 1960-1972." INTERNATIONAL ORGANIZATION 27 (Autumn 1973): 431-64.

A study of how political and economic factors influenced international monetary reforms of the 1960s. The author suggests that transgovernmental interaction among central banks and finance ministries of the major industrial states was as important in international monetary system developments as direct governmental interaction.

Schmiegelow, Henrik, and Schmiegelow, Michele. "The New Mercantilism in International Relations: The Case of France's External Monetary Policy." INTERNATIONAL ORGANIZATION 29 (Spring 1975): 367-92.

Shonfield, Andrew. "Towards an International Currency." INTERNATIONAL AFFAIRS 43 (January 1967): 39-50.

A historical analysis of some of the problems and tensions relating to the expansion of international monetary reserves.

Stevens, Robert. A PRIMER ON THE DOLLAR IN THE WORLD ECONOMY; UNITED STATES BALANCE OF PAYMENTS AND INTERNATIONAL MONETARY REFORM. New York: Random House, 1972. vi, 232 p.

An excellent introduction to the relationship of the U.S. economy to the international monetary system. The appendix includes a short chronology of the major balance of payments issues and problems from 1958 to 1971.

Strange, Susan. "The Dollar Crisis of 1971." INTERNATIONAL AFFAIRS 48 (April 1972): 191-215.

An account of the international monetary crisis of 1971 and how it was temporarily resolved. The first part of the article analyzes shortcomings of political science and economics in handling the interdisciplinary problems of the international system.

_____. "The Politics of International Currencies." WORLD POLITICS 23 (January 1971): 215-31.

Sets forth a political theory of international currencies and then attempts to apply it to the international monetary problems of the late 1960s.

Triffin, Robert. OUR INTERNATIONAL MONETARY SYSTEM; YESTERDAY, TODAY AND TOMORROW. New York: Random House, 1968. xvi, 206 p.

Sketches the historical evolution of the international monetary system from 1815 to 1965 and analyzes alternative reform plans for improving the contemporary system.

Viner, Jacob. "Political Aspects of International Finance." JOURNAL OF BUSINESS 1 (April 1928): 141-73; (July 1928): 324-63.

The relationship of politics to international finance is examined by analyzing four themes: government techniques for promoting capital exports; political restrictions on capital exports; governmental promotion of foreign loans; and the pursuit of international finance objectives through political means.

Chapter 6
POLITICS AND FOREIGN AID

Foreign aid, the process of transferring economic, military, or other real resources
to foreign states, has been an important dimension of the postwar foreign policies of most developed states. Although humanitarian considerations have been
a guiding purpose for granting such assistance, political concerns have also
been of central importance. Moreover, the process of developing aid programs
has involved domestic political processes in the grantor state, while domestic
political interests of the grantee state have played an important role in the
distribution of such aid. Politics, in short, has been a part of the aid-giving
and aid-receiving process. In this chapter we shall examine (in part one) some
of the significant literature on the political economy of foreign aid and then
(in the second and third parts) review some of the studies on the bilateral assistance of the United States and of other developed states.

A. THE ECONOMICS AND POLITICS OF AID

Asher, Robert E. "Development Assistance in D.D.II: The Recommendations
of Perkins, Pearson, Peterson, Prebisch, and Others." INTERNATIONAL ORGA-
NIZATION 25 (Winter 1971): 97-119.

> An analysis of the major aid reports of the late 1960s and early
> 1970s and a discussion of the critical operational problems in de-
> veloping a new foreign aid program in the United States.

_____. "Economic Co-operation under U.N. Auspices." INTERNATIONAL
ORGANIZATION 12 (Summer 1958): 288-302.

> Examines the increasing role international organizations have played
> in the economic development of the LDCs and presents some pros
> and cons of multilateral aid.

_____. GRANTS, LOANS, AND LOCAL CURRENCIES: THEIR ROLE IN
FOREIGN AID. Washington, D.C.: Brookings Institution, 1961. 135 p.

> A forthright discussion of grants and loans and the relative merits
> of each in transferring economic assistance to the LDCs. Asher

also examines the impact of foreign aid on the balance of payments of both donor and recipient countries and some of the major policy problems involved in determining the need for aid and the means for transferring it.

Bernstein, S.J., and Alpert, E.J. "Foreign Aid and Voting Behavior in the U.N.: The Admission of Communist China." ORBIS 15 (Fall 1971): 963-77.

Bhagwati, Jagdish N. AMOUNT AND SHARING OF AID. Washington, D.C.: Overseas Development Council, 1970. 197 p.

Bhagwati, Jagdish N., and Eckaus, Richard S., eds. FOREIGN AID: SELECTED READINGS. London: Penguin Books, 1970. 351 p.

An excellent collection of readings dealing primarily with economic issues of foreign aid.

Black, Eugene R. THE DIPLOMACY OF ECONOMIC DEVELOPMENT. Cambridge, Mass.: Harvard University Press, 1961. 74 p.

Black, a former president of the World Bank, pleas for the establishment of a distinct development diplomacy--a diplomacy that will help the LDCs become more economically developed. These essays were originally given as the William L. Clayton Lectures at the Fletcher School of Law and Diplomacy.

Black, Lloyd A. THE STRATEGY OF FOREIGN AID. Princeton, N.J.: Van Nostrand, 1968. xiii, 176 p.

Black, a geography professor, discusses the objectives, methods, and effects of foreign aid.

Dillon, Wilton. GIFTS AND NATIONS; THE OBLIGATION TO GIVE, RECEIVE AND REPAY. The Hague: Mouton, 1968. 113 p.

Dublin, Jack. "Foreign Assistance Through Private Enterprise: A New Challenge to U.S. Credit Unions and Other Cooperatives." JOURNAL OF INTERNATIONAL LAW AND ECONOMICS 6 (June 1971): 25-57.

A discussion of the possibilities of increasing U.S. economic aid through the private sector, particularly through credit unions.

Eldridge, P.J. THE POLITICS OF FOREIGN AID IN INDIA. New York: Schocken Press, 1970. xx, 389 p.

Examines the aid policies and programs of the United States and the Soviet Union in India and attempts to assess the political impact of such aid, particularly assistance in the form of food, oil, and steel industries.

Feldman, Herbert. "Aid as Imperialism?" INTERNATIONAL AFFAIRS 43 (April 1967): 219-35.

> Feldman finds that there are three major weaknesses in the countries receiving aid: poor leadership, corruption, and lack of will to improve. Because of political and economic weaknesses in the LDCs, Feldman foresees the possible resurgence of imperialism through the aid-granting process.

Friedmann, Wolfgang; Kalmanoff, George; and Meagher, Robert F. INTERNATIONAL FINANCIAL AID. New York: Columbia University Press, 1966. 498 p.

> A general overview of types, methods, purposes, and effects of aid illuminated by numerous case studies.

Gordenker, Leon. "Multilateral Aid and Influence on Government Policies." In THE POLITICS OF INTERNATIONAL ORGANIZATIONS, edited by Robert W. Cox, pp. 128-52. New York: Praeger Publishers, 1970.

> An analysis of how and under what conditions international organizations may influence domestic policies in the aid-receiving countries. This short study focuses on the U.N. Development Program and its operation in Malawi, Tanzania, and Zambia.

Griffin, Keith B., and Enos, John L. "Foreign Assistance: Objectives and Consequences." ECONOMIC DEVELOPMENT AND CULTURAL CHANGE 18 (April 1970): 313-27.

> The authors explore some of the consequences of aid and find that economic aid is not statistically correlated with economic growth. Their thesis is that aid supplants rather than supplements domestic investment.

Gutteridge, William F. "The Impact of Foreign Aid upon the Political Role of the Armed Forces in Developing Countries." In THE POLITICS OF INTERNATIONAL ORGANIZATIONS, edited by Robert W. Cox, pp. 217-26. New York: Praeger Publishers, 1970.

> Suggests that it is virtually impossible to determine the effect of foreign aid on domestic politics. The rise of militarism is the result chiefly of domestic conditions, although foreign military assistance may affect the direction and type of development of the armed forces.

Hawkins, Edward K. THE PRINCIPLES OF DEVELOPMENT AID. London: Penguin Books, 1970. 135 p.

> A short, introductory volume on economic aid, focusing on its sources, form, and quantity.

Hayter, Teresa. AID AS IMPERIALISM. Baltimore: Penguin Books, 1971. 213 p.

> This controversial study, originally commissioned by the Overseas Development Institute, argues that economic aid is simply a tool for preserving the capitalist system in the LDCs. Hayter examines the policies, rationale, and methods of the aid programs of the World Bank, IMF, AID, and the Inter-American Committee for the Alliance for Progress, and then reviews the performance of these agencies in Colombia, Chile, Brazil, and Peru.

Hudson, Michael, and Goulet, Dennis. THE MYTH OF AID; THE HIDDEN AGENDA OF DEVELOPMENT REPORTS. Prepared by Center for the Study of Development and Social Change. New York: IDOC North America, 1971. 135 p.

> The authors suggest that traditional economic aid is only a palliative, not a cure, to the increasing structural inequities between rich and poor countries. Goulet's essay examines and critiques the underlying assumptions of the U.S. foreign aid program, while Hudson's essay focuses on the political dimension of the U.S. and World Bank programs.

Mende, Tibor. FROM AID TO RE-COLONIZATION: LESSONS OF A FAILURE. New York: Pantheon Books, 1973. 317 p.

> Examines the dynamics of the relationship of the industrial countries to the LDCs over the postwar years, and attempts to explain why the Third World has not developed economically.

Mikesell, Raymond F. THE ECONOMICS OF FOREIGN AID. Chicago: Aldine Publishing Co., 1968. 282 p.

> A comprehensive analysis of the economic principles and issues relating to foreign aid.

Montgomery, John D. FOREIGN AID IN INTERNATIONAL POLITICS. Englewood Cliffs, N.J.: Prentice-Hall, 1967. 106 p.

> A short introductory study of the subject of foreign economic assistance. An annotated bibliography is included.

Morgenthau, Hans. "A Political Theory of Foreign Aid." AMERICAN POLITICAL SCIENCE REVIEW 56 (June 1962): 301-9.

> The noted political scientist sketches six types of aid--humanitarian, subsistence, military, bribery, prestige, and economic development. He argues that an effective theory of aid must differentiate between the various types and establish programs whose methods are consistent with its objectives.

Ohlin, Goran. FOREIGN AID POLICIES RECONSIDERED. Paris: Development Centre of the Organization for Economic Cooperation and Development, 1966. 120 p.

> A general overview of the politics and economics of foreign aid. See particularly chapter 3, "Public Opinion and Foreign Aid."

Papanek, Gustav F. "Aid, Foreign Private Investment, and Growth in Less Developed Countries." JOURNAL OF POLITICAL ECONOMY 81 (January-February 1973): 120-30.

Pearson, Lester B., et al. PARTNERS IN DEVELOPMENT; REPORT OF THE COMMISSION ON INTERNATIONAL DEVELOPMENT. New York: Praeger Publishers, 1969. 395 p.

> This report, prepared by a group of noted economists, suggests that economic aid to the LDCs must be increased if the gap between the developed and underdeveloped states is to be closed. Policy recommendations are offered not only on bilateral aid but on private foreign investment, trade, debt repayment, and family planning. The annex includes a useful assessment of the economic development situation of the different regions of the world as of 1969.

Pincus, John. ECONOMIC AID AND INTERNATIONAL COST-SHARING. Baltimore: Johns Hopkins Press, 1965. 193 p.

> A thorough and sophisticated study of the economics of burden sharing of economic aid to the LDCs. Sharing the costs of aid is important, according to Pincus, because all developed countries benefit from the positive effects of aid from donor countries. Unfortunately, there is no completely equitable method of sharing aid costs.

_____. TRADE, AID AND DEVELOPMENT: THE RICH AND POOR NATIONS. New York: McGraw-Hill Book Co., 1967. 376 p.

> An excellent discussion of some of the main theoretical and policy issues between the rich and poor nations. The policy analysis focuses on trade of manufactures, commodity agreements, and aid.

Sumberg, Theodore A. FOREIGN AID AS A MORAL OBLIGATION? Beverly Hills, Calif.: Sage Publications, 1973. 72 p.

> Sets forth a moral rationale for foreign aid.

Thorp, Willard L. THE REALITY OF FOREIGN AID. Published for the Council on Foreign Relations. New York: Praeger Publishers, 1971. 350 p.

> A general study of the theory and practice of economic aid, with particular emphasis on purposes and processes.

Wall, David. THE CHARITY OF NATIONS; THE POLITICAL ECONOMY OF AID. New York: Basic Books, 1973. 181 p.

> This careful, up-to-date study of the political dimensions of foreign aid examines the objectives, methods, and problems of the aid programs of Western democracies. Chapter 4 deals with the domestic political process of aid allocation.

Ward, Barbara. "Foreign Aid: Strategy or Stopgap." FOREIGN AFFAIRS 41 (October 1962): 90-104.

> Ward argues that aid is an essential instrument for Western security as well as an essential need for the LDC economies.

Ward, Barbara, et al., eds. THE WIDENING GAP; DEVELOPMENT IN THE 1970'S. New York: Columbia University Press, 1971. xi, 372 p.

> A series of papers prepared for the Columbia Conference on International Economic Development of February 1970. The conference was convened to discuss implications of the Pearson Commission Report.

White, John A. THE POLITICS OF FOREIGN AID. London: Bodley Head, 1974. 316 p.

Wiggins, James W., and Schoeck, Helmut, eds. FOREIGN AID REEXAMINED, A CRITICAL APPRAISAL. Washington, D.C.: Public Affairs Press, 1958. 250 p.

> A collection of fourteen essays, originally prepared for a conference at Emory University, on the purposes and methods of foreign aid as a tool for economic development.

Wittkopf, E.R. "Foreign Aid and U.N. Votes: A Comparative Study." AMERICAN POLITICAL SCIENCE REVIEW 67 (September 1973): 868-88.

> An analysis of the relationship between U.N. voting behavior and economic assistance. The study found that there was a positive correlation between the two variables for the United States, although the causal connection between aid and voting behavior is unknown.

B. U.S. FOREIGN AID

Baldwin, David A. ECONOMIC DEVELOPMENT AND AMERICAN FOREIGN POLICY, 1943-62. Chicago: University of Chicago Press, 1966. 272 p.

> A study on how and why the United States came to adopt "soft" loans as the principal means of encouraging economic growth in the LDCs. A general bibliography on economic aid is appended.

_____. FOREIGN AID AND AMERICAN FOREIGN POLICY: A DOCUMEN-
TARY ANALYSIS. New York: Praeger Publishers, 1966. 257 p.

A useful collection of reports, articles, and statements on various
issues of U.S. economic aid, such as grants versus loans, multilateral versus bilateral aid, military versus economic aid, the relationship of aid to trade, and foreign investment and the American economy.

Banfield, Edward C. AMERICAN FOREIGN AID DOCTRINES. Washington,
D.C.: American Enterprise Institute for Public Policy Research, January 1963.
65 p.

An analysis of the doctrines used to justify American aid. Banfield argues that there has been no rational, consistent, systematic
theory for U.S. aid largely because the American democratic experience is one based on optimism, moralism, and the goodness of
democracy.

Bird, Richard M. "What's Wrong with the United States Foreign Aid Programme?"
INTERNATIONAL JOURNAL 25 (1969-70): 9-22.

The major weakness of the U.S. aid program is that "far too much
has been attempted with far too little."

Brown, Lester R., and Eckholm, Erik P. "Food: Growing Global Insecurity."
In THE U.S. AND THE DEVELOPING WORLD: AGENDA FOR ACTION, 1974,
edited by James W. Howe, pp. 66-84. New York: Praeger Publishers, 1974.

Discusses the food problem in the developing countries and some
possible strategies for assisting those nations.

Brown, William Adams, Jr., and Opie, Redvers. AMERICAN FOREIGN ASSIS-
TANCE. Washington, D.C.: Brookings Institution, 1953. 598 p.

The definitive early history of American foreign assistance, focusing
on the postwar economic and military assistance programs.

Chandrasekhar, Sripati. AMERICAN AID AND INDIA'S ECONOMIC DEVELOP-
MENT, 1951-1964. New York: Praeger Publishers, 1966. x, 243 p.

A sympathetic account of the U.S. foreign aid program in India.

Cleveland, Harlan. THE THEORY AND PRACTICE OF FOREIGN AID; A
PAPER PREPARED FOR THE SPECIAL STUDIES PROJECT OF THE ROCKEFELLER
BROTHERS FUND. Syracuse, N.Y.: Maxwell Graduate School of Citizenship
and Public Affairs, Syracuse University, 1956. 93 p.

A short, lucid study of the means, objectives, and results of foreign economic assistance. Cleveland offers suggestions on how
U.S. aid can be made more effective.

Feis, Herbert. FOREIGN AID AND FOREIGN POLICY. New York: St. Martin's Press, 1964. 240 p.

> A general, somewhat journalistic account of the political economy of U.S. aid. Chapters 4 and 5 give a brief historical sketch of the relationship of economic assistance to foreign policy.

Frank, Charles R., Jr., and Baird, Mary. "Foreign Aid: Its Speckled Past and Future Prospects." INTERNATIONAL ORGANIZATION 29 (Winter 1975): 133-67.

> The authors suggest that the U.S. foreign aid program should be differentiated into several smaller programs each of which would have a more precise set of objectives. In addition, the authors argue that humanitarian and economic development aid should be multiloteralized, while strategic military and economic assistance should continue in bilateral form.

Hamilton, Edward K. "Toward Public Confidence in Foreign Aid." WORLD AFFAIRS 132 (March 1970): 287-304.

Haviland, H. Field, Jr. "Foreign Aid and the Policy Process: 1957." AMERICAN POLITICAL SCIENCE REVIEW 52 (September 1958): 689-724.

> An analysis of the 1957 Congressional debate regarding the U.S. economic aid program.

Huntington, Samuel. "Foreign Aid: For What and For Whom?" FOREIGN POLICY, no. 1 (Winter 1970-71): 161-89.

> United States economic aid programs should be based on national interests, and since the economic development of the LDCs is one such interest, the United States should continue to supply aid to the needy states.

_____. "Foreign Aid: For What and For Whom?" FOREIGN POLICY, no. 2 (Spring 1971): 114-34.

> Huntington discusses some of the major objectives of the U.S. aid program and suggests that the only effective way of implementing programs with different objectives is to disaggregate the unified aid program and establish several smaller ones.

Jacoby, Neil H. U.S. AID TO TAIWAN: A STUDY OF FOREIGN AID, SELF-HELP, AND DEVELOPMENT. New York: Praeger Publishers, 1967. xviii, 364 p.

> A case study of U.S. economic assistance to Taiwan, with emphasis on the effect on the development process.

Johnson, Bruce F. "Farm Surpluses and Foreign Policy." WORLD POLITICS 10 (October 1957): 1-23.

Discusses some of the possible uses of farm surpluses in the foreign aid program.

Jordan, Amos A. FOREIGN AID AND THE DEFENSE OF SOUTHEAST ASIA. New York: Praeger Publishers, 1962. 272 p.

Examines the political and economic dimensions of the U.S. aid program in seven South and Southeast Asian countries.

Kaplan, Jacob J. THE CHALLENGE OF FOREIGN AID; POLICIES, PROBLEMS AND POSSIBILITIES. New York: Praeger Publishers, 1967. 399 p.

Evaluates the U.S. aid program with a view of developing policies that are more effective in carrying out the real interests of the American people. Chapter 7 examines the relationship of foreign aid to the "durable U.S. interests."

Krassowski, Andrzej. THE AID RELATIONSHIP: A DISCUSSION OF AID STRATEGY WITH EXAMPLES FROM THE AMERICAN EXPERIENCE IN TUNISIA. London: Overseas Development Institute, 1968. 121 p.

An informative study of the administrative institutions and processes involved in the U.S. aid program. The study focuses on the U.S. program in Tunisia.

Liska, George. THE NEW STATECRAFT; FOREIGN AID IN AMERICAN FOR-EIGN POLICY. Chicago: University of Chicago Press, 1960. 246 p.

Attempts to develop a political theory of foreign aid by examining the relationship of aid to foreign policy.

Lodge, George C. "U.S. Aid to Latin America: Funding Radical Change." FOREIGN AFFAIRS 47 (July 1969): 735-49.

Suggests that U.S. aid be distributed through two channels for two distinct purposes. The first type of aid would be distributed through multilateral organizations to encourage economic growth in the LDCs; the second type of aid would be distributed through a non-governmental, independent foundation to develop new "growth structures" and local organizations which could exert pressure for radical change on the existing system. Lodge suggests that about 70 percent of the aid be distributed through the first channel and about 25 through the second.

Loeber, Thomas S. FOREIGN AID: OUR TRAGIC EXPERIMENT. New York: W.W. Norton, 1961. 139 p.

Describes corruption and mismanagement of the early U.S. foreign aid program.

Mason, Edward S. FOREIGN AID AND FOREIGN POLICY. Published for the Council on Foreign Relations. New York: Harper & Row, 1964. ix, 118 p.

> The Elihu Root Lectures of the Council on Foreign Relations given in May 1963.

Mikesell, Raymond F. "America's Economic Responsibilities as a Great Power." AMERICAN ECONOMIC REVIEW: PAPERS AND PROCEEDINGS 1 (May 1952): 258-70.

Millikan, Max F., and Rostow, W.W. A PROPOSAL: KEY TO AN EFFEC-TIVE FOREIGN POLICY. New York: Harper & Brothers, 1957. 170 p.

> A pioneering study on the relationship of economic aid to the development of stable, politically mature nations. The authors point to some fallacies of economic assistance and develop a clear rationale for an effective American foreign policy. The proposal helped refine the U.S. aid legislation of 1961.

Montgomery, John D. THE POLITICS OF FOREIGN AID; AMERICAN EXPE-RIENCE IN SOUTHEAST ASIA. Published for the Council on Foreign Relations. New York: Praeger Publishers, 1962. 321 p.

> Based on his analysis of the U.S. foreign aid program in Southeast Asia, Montgomery argues that a flexible decentralized approach is the most effective means of ensuring that aid is distributed wisely. Aid programs must be adapted to the particular conditions and needs of a country if they are to be effective in encouraging economic development.

Moomaw, I.W. THE CHALLENGE OF HUNGER; A PROGRAM FOR MORE EFFECTIVE FOREIGN AID. New York: Praeger Publishers, 1966. xiii, 222 p.

> A general analysis of the objectives and methods of the U.S. for-eign aid program.

Nelson, Joan M. AID, INFLUENCE, AND FOREIGN POLICY. New York: Macmillan Co., 1968. 149 p.

> Examines the goals, programs, and potential sources of influence in the American aid program. Chapters 5 and 6 discuss the short- and long-run political objectives of economic assistance.

O'Leary, Michael K. THE POLITICS OF AMERICAN FOREIGN AID. New York: Atherton Press, 1967. xiv, 172 p.

> The best study on the domestic politics of the U.S. aid program. O'Leary examines the impact of political culture, public opinion, the Congress, and the President on the development of aid policies.

Packenham, Robert A. "Foreign Aid and the National Interest." MIDWEST JOURNAL OF POLITICAL SCIENCE 10 (May 1966): 214-21.

Based on interviews with foreign policy officials at the Department of State, Packenham's conclusion is that the guiding rationale for the U.S. aid program is the national interest, not humanitarian concerns.

_____. LIBERAL AMERICA AND THE THIRD WORLD. Princeton, N.J.: Princeton University Press, 1973. 378 p.

An analysis of how the liberal, optimistic tradition in the United States has affected the development of foreign aid doctrines as well as the theories of American social scientists. Chapters 1 and 2 are an excellent summary of the U.S. political development doctrines of the 1947-68 period.

_____. "Political-Development Doctrines in the American Foreign Aid Program." WORLD POLITICS 18 (January 1966): 194-235.

Interviewing government aid officials, the author found that there was a significant discrepancy between the declared political objectives of U.S. aid programs and their actual implementation. The author offers several tentative explanations for the gap between objectives and performance.

Palmer, N[orman].D. "Foreign Aid and Foreign Policy: The New Statecraft Reassessed." ORBIS 13 (Fall 1969): 763-82.

A general discussion of the relationship of aid to foreign policy.

Roett, Riordan. THE POLITICS OF FOREIGN AID IN THE BRAZILIAN NORTH-EAST. Nashville, Tenn.: Vanderbilt University Press, 1972. xii, 202 p.

Roett suggests that the U.S. aid program in northeastern Brazil has had limited impact on the region's economic development and that it has tended to strengthen the power of the traditional oligarchy instead.

Rosenfield, Stephen S. "The Politics of Food." FOREIGN POLICY, no. 14 (Spring 1974): 17-29.

A short study of the political forces behind the U.S. policy toward the world food shortage of the early 1970s.

Thompson, Kenneth W. FOREIGN ASSISTANCE: A VIEW FROM THE PRIVATE SECTOR. Notre Dame, Ind.: University of Notre Dame Press, 1972. 160 p.

Examines some private American efforts to assist the LDCs in such areas as health, agriculture, and education.

U.S. Task Force on International Development. U.S. FOREIGN ASSISTANCE IN THE 1970'S: A NEW APPROACH. Washington, D.C.: Government Printing Office, 1970. 39 p.

> A group of distinguished Americans offer suggestions on how to improve the effectiveness of the U.S. aid program.

Weissman, Steve R., and members of Pacific Studies Center and the North American Congress on Latin America. THE TROJAN HORSE: A RADICAL LOOK AT FOREIGN AID. San Francisco: Ramparts Press, 1974. 249 p.

> A polemical attack on the U.S. foreign aid program by a group of "radical" writers who believe that the aid process is simply a tool for controlling the peoples of the LDCs.

Wolf, Charles, Jr. FOREIGN AID: THEORY AND PRACTICE IN SOUTHERN ASIA. Princeton, N.J.: Princeton University Press, 1960. 416 p.

> A pioneer study of U.S. aid that sets forth a theory for the efficient allocation of military and economic assistance. A large part of the study is devoted to a historical analysis of the Southern Asia aid program.

C. OTHER BILATERAL AID

Amir, Shimeon. ISRAEL'S DEVELOPMENT COOPERATION WITH AFRICA, ASIA, AND LATIN AMERICA. New York: Praeger Publishers, 1974. xvi, 133 p.

> Amir describes Israel's economic assistance program, which he heads.

Arnold, H.J.P. AID FOR DEVELOPING COUNTRIES, A COMPARATIVE STUDY. Chester Springs, Pa.: Dufour Editions; London: Bodley Head, 1962. 159 p.

> A general survey of the economic aid programs of the United States, the Soviet Union, Great Britain, Western Europe, and selected international organizations as of 1959.

Berliner, Joseph S. SOVIET ECONOMIC AID: THE NEW AID AND TRADE POLICY IN UNDERDEVELOPED NATIONS. Published for the Council on Foreign Relations. New York: Praeger Publishers, 1958. 323 p.

> A careful examination and assessment of the Soviet Union's foreign aid programs of the 1950s. The author focuses on the methods and purposes of the aid programs as well as on their relationship to political institutions and processes.

Billerbeck, Klaus. SOVIET BLOC FOREIGN AID TO UNDERDEVELOPED COUNTRIES: AN ANALYSIS AND PROGNOSIS. Hamburg, Germany:

Archives of World Economy, 1960. 161 p.

A balanced and systematic study of the early aid program of the Soviet Union.

Goldman, Marshall I. SOVIET FOREIGN AID. New York: Praeger Publishers, 1967. 258 p.

Probably the most thorough study of the Soviet Union's economic relations with the LDCs. Each of chapters 2 through 10 examines Soviet assistance to selected nations and regions, while chapter 11 summarizes the purposes, methods, and accomplishments of the aid program.

Hart, Judith. AID AND LIBERATION; A SOCIALIST STUDY OF AID POLICIES. London: Gollancz, 1973. 287 p.

Hart, a former British Labor Party Minister of Overseas Development, discusses the needs of Third World countries and how the developed countries can assist in their development. In chapter 9 the author presents a list of recommendations for establishing a British Socialist aid program which would more effectively transfer economic resources to the poor states.

Herman, Leon M. "The Political Goals of Soviet Foreign Aid." In HEARINGS BEFORE THE SUBCOMMITTEE OF FOREIGN ECONOMIC POLICY OF THE JOINT ECONOMIC COMMITTEE, 84th Cong., 2d sess., December 1956, pp. 475-85. Washington, D.C.: Government Printing Office, 1957.

A brief discussion of the Soviet Union's principal ideological objectives in its cold war foreign aid program.

Heymann, Hans, Jr. "Soviet Foreign Aid as a Problem for U.S. Policy." WORLD POLITICS 12 (July 1960): 525-40.

Heymann, a RAND Corporation economist, examines some of the major differences between the U.S. and USSR aid programs and suggests that the United States ought to counteract the popularity of the Soviet programs by developing a more effective program.

Jones, David. EUROPE'S CHOSEN FEW: POLICY AND PRACTICE OF THE EEC AID PROGRAMME. London: Overseas Development Institute, 1973. 99 p.

Kreinin, Mordechai E. ISRAEL AND AFRICA, A STUDY IN TECHNICAL CO-OPERATION. New York: Praeger Publishers, 1964. 206 p.

Examines Israel's aid programs to Asian and African countries, especially those programs related to agriculture and education.

Laufer, Leopold. ISRAEL AND THE DEVELOPING COUNTRIES: NEW AP-

PROACHES TO COOPERATION. New York: Twentieth Century Fund, 1967. 298 p.

A study of Israel's informal foreign aid program during the 1956-67 period.

Little, I.M.D. AID TO AFRICA, AN APPRAISAL OF U.K. POLICY FOR AID TO AFRICA SOUTH OF THE SAHARA. Oxford: Pergamon Press; New York: Macmillan Co., 1964.

Little, I.M.D., and Clifford, J. INTERNATIONAL AID; A DISCUSSION OF THE FLOW OF PUBLIC RESOURCES FROM RICH TO POOR COUNTRIES, WITH PARTICULAR REFERENCE TO BRITISH POLICY. London: George Allen & Unwin, 1965. 338 p.

A general examination of the principles, processes, and problems involved in giving economic aid. Part 4 of the study deals with British assistance and offers some suggestions for improving methods of distribution.

Mihaly, Eugene B. FOREIGN AID AND POLITICS IN NEPAL; A CASE STUDY. London: Oxford University Press, 1965. 202 p.

A study of the domestic politics of foreign economic aid in Nepal during the period 1951-62. The study examines aid projects from the United States, the Soviet Union, China, Switzerland, India, and Israel.

Muller, Kurt. THE FOREIGN AID PROGRAMS OF THE SOVIET BLOC AND COMMUNIST CHINA. Translated by Richard H. Weber and Michael Roloff. New York: Walker & Co., 1964. 331 p.

Pye, Lucian. "Soviet and American Styles in Foreign Aid." ORBIS 4 (Summer 1960): 159-73.

A comparative analysis of the U.S. and Soviet aid programs of the 1950s. Pye suggests that the American programs are far more sophisticated than those of the Soviet Union, but that the latter's are better integrated with its foreign policy.

Radetzki, Marian. AID AND DEVELOPMENT: A HANDBOOK FOR SMALL DONORS. New York: Praeger Publishers, 1973. xxiv, 323 p.

An excellent case study of Sweden's economic assistance programs. Based on a careful review of the impact of its national and regional programs, the author suggests that the effectiveness of aid would be improved if it were not "tied" and if it were accompanied by international technical assistance.

Reuber, Grant L. "The Trade-Offs Among Objectives of Canadian Foreign

Aid." INTERNATIONAL JOURNAL 25 (Winter 1969-70): 129-41.

Walters, Robert S. AMERICAN AND SOVIET AID: A COMPARATIVE ANALY-
SIS. Pittsburgh: University of Pittsburgh Press, 1970. xiii, 299 p.

A comprehensive comparative analysis of the economic aid programs
of the Soviet Union and the United States. The study focuses on
the purposes, scope, organization, and dynamics of the assistance
programs.

Chapter 7

FOREIGN PRIVATE INVESTMENT

Foreign private investment involves the direct transfer of capital and technology by private business firms from one state to another. Although such transfers are normally a private business transaction, large continuous transfers are of public concern because of their political and economic implications for both host and parent countries. As a result, host governments attempt to regulate the entry of foreign investment, while parent governments may attempt to influence or control the exportation of capital or set up guidelines to protect their nation's foreign investments. A particularly important contemporary development has been the rise of the MNC, which poses a political and economic challenge not only to the LDCs but also to the developed states and the international system itself. This chapter examines the significant literature on the political economy of foreign investment. The first part focuses on the literature concerning general bilateral foreign investment, while the second part deals with the MNC.

A. THE POLITICAL ECONOMY OF FOREIGN INVESTMENT

Aitken, Thomas, Jr. A FOREIGN POLICY FOR AMERICAN BUSINESS. New York: Harper Brothers, 1962. 159 p.

> In chapter 12 of this short, readable volume the author examines the relationship of foreign investment to American foreign policy. He suggests that since American business is a part of U.S. foreign policy it is imperative that government and the business community cooperate in both making and implementing foreign policy.

Baer, Werner, and Simonsen, Mario. "American Capital and Brazilian Nationalism." YALE REVIEW 53 (December 1963): 192-98.

> An examination of the Brazilian response to U.S. foreign invest-ment. The writers attempt to explain the increasing negative re-sponse to such investment, given the important economic benefits that have accrued from foreign capital.

Behrman, Jack N. U.S. INTERNATIONAL BUSINESS AND GOVERNMENTS. New York: McGraw-Hill Book Co., 1971. 244 p.

A general descriptive account of the relationship of U.S. foreign business to home and host governments.

Bernstein, Marvin, ed. FOREIGN INVESTMENT IN LATIN AMERICA: CASES AND ATTITUDES. New York: Alfred A. Knopf, 1966. 305 p.

A fine collection of readings on U.S. foreign investment in Latin America. A helpful bibliographical essay is included.

Blanchard, Daniel S. "The Threat to U.S. Private Investment in Latin America." JOURNAL OF INTERNATIONAL LAW AND ECONOMICS 5 (January 1971): 221-37.

Blanchard suggests that, given increasing pressures to expropriate U.S. investments in Latin America, joint ventures may be the most effective method of countering complete loss of control and ownership.

Bronfenbrenner, Martin. "The Appeal of Confiscation in Economic Development." ECONOMIC DEVELOPMENT AND CULTURAL CHANGE 3 (April 1955): 201-18.

Sets forth the economic benefits of expropriation.

Davis, S.Sm. "U.S. Versus Latin America: Business and Culture." HARVARD BUSINESS REVIEW 47 (November-December 1969): 88-98.

American foreign enterprise in Latin America can increase its performance by adapting their operations to the culture of host countries.

Engler, Robert. THE POLITICS OF OIL: A STUDY OF PRIVATE POWER AND DEMOCRATIC DIRECTIONS. New York: Macmillan Co., 1961. 565 p.

A lengthy, descriptive account of the relationship of oil corporations to the U.S. government. Citing the increasing economic and political power of the oil industry which threatens American democracy, Engler argues that the U.S. government must institute planning to direct and regulate the behavior of the oil companies.

Gilpin, Robert. U.S. POWER AND THE MULTINATIONAL CORPORATION: THE POLITICAL ECONOMY OF FOREIGN DIRECT INVESTMENT. New York: Basic Books, 1975. xii, 291 p.

The era of Pax Americana is coming to an end as power becomes more widely dispersed within the international system. The United States must therefore reevaluate its strategy toward direct foreign investment if its political and economic national interests are to be maximized. Because of the decreasing influence of the United States in the world, Gilpin believes that it is unwise to continue to rely heavily on foreign direct investment as a means of meeting foreign competition, earning foreign exchange, and solving domes-

tic economic problems. Besides the valuable policy recommendations offered in chapter 8 for the creation of an alternative strategy for U.S. foreign investment, Gilpin's study (particularly in
chapter 2) provides one of the most succinct and lucid discussions
of the field of international political economy. This volume is
essential reading for anyone concerned with the relationship of
international politics to the MNC in general and to U.S. foreign
investment in particular.

Goodman, Bernard. "The Political Economy of Private International Investment."
ECONOMIC DEVELOPMENT AND CULTURAL CHANGE 5 (April 1957): 263-76.

> Goodman argues that indiscriminate foreign investment in the LDCs
> may have important long-term political disadvantages for the United
> States.

Grunwald, Joseph. "Foreign Private Investment: The Challenge of Latin America Nationalism." VIRGINIA JOURNAL OF INTERNATIONAL LAW 11 (March
1971): 228-45.

> Tries to explain some of the negative attitudes of Latin Americans
> toward U.S. foreign investment. Grunwald offers several policy
> recommendations designed to appease Latinos.

Hartshorn, J.E. POLITICS AND WORLD OIL ECONOMICS: AN ACCOUNT
OF THE INTERNATIONAL OIL INDUSTRY IN ITS POLITICAL ENVIRONMENT.
Rev. ed. New York: Praeger Publishers, 1967. 404 p.

> Despite its title, this is primarily a descriptive account of oil--
> where it is produced and consumed, the role and operation of oil
> industries, and the economics of production.

Hirschman, Albert O. HOW TO DIVEST IN LATIN AMERICA AND WHY.
Princeton Essays in International Finance, no. 76. Princeton, N.J.: International Finance Section, Department of Economics, Princeton University, 1969.
24 p.

> The noted political economist and student of Latin American af-
> fairs argues that direct foreign investment is a "mixed" blessing.
> He presents a number of suggestions on how to transfer partial owner-
> ship of foreign companies to local interests. For a refutation of Hirsch-
> man's position, see Virgil Salera's essay (below, this section).

Hoskins, William R. "How To Counter Expropriation." HARVARD BUSINESS
REVIEW 48 (September-October 1970): 102-12.

> Reviews some of the available methods of obtaining compensation
> after expropriation. Since none of the methods examined is com-
> pletely fruitful, Hoskins believes that the capital-exporting and
> capital-importing states should develop an international legal sys-
> tem that can deal more effectively with the problems of expropria-
> tion.

Hunter, John M. "Long-Term Foreign Investment and Underdeveloped Countries." JOURNAL OF POLITICAL ECONOMY 61 (February 1953): 15-24.

Analyzes the important political and economic factors related to long-term profitability of foreign investment.

Kidron, Michael. FOREIGN INVESTMENTS IN INDIA. New York: Oxford University Press, 1965. 368 p.

Kidron examines and attempts to explain the historical development of Indian attitudes and policies toward foreign investment. An excellent case study of the relationship of foreign investment firms to host governments.

Kindleberger, Charles P. AMERICAN BUSINESS ABROAD; SIX LECTURES ON DIRECT INVESTMENT. New Haven, Conn.: Yale University Press, 1969. 210 p.

A balanced theoretical analysis of the economics of direct foreign investment.

Lenczowski, George. OIL AND STATE IN THE MIDDLE EAST. Ithaca, N.Y.: Cornell University Press, 1960. xix, 379 p.

One of the best descriptive accounts of the early development of the oil industry in the Middle East. Part 1 examines the economic role of oil in European and Middle Eastern economies; parts 2 to 4 analyze the oil industry's relations with host governments, the public in host countries, and its foreign employees. Particularly useful is the analysis of the domestic politics of foreign oil development in chapters 4-10.

Levy, Walter J. "World Oil Cooperation or International Chaos." FOREIGN AFFAIRS 52 (July 1974): 690-713.

Levy, an oil consultant, suggests that the only effective way for oil-importing nations to deal with the oil policies of OPEC is through cooperation and coordination. In addition, oil-importing states must establish energy austerity programs as well as attempt to understand the interests and aspirations of the producing states.

Litvak, Isaiah A., and Maule, Christopher J., eds. FOREIGN INVESTMENT: THE EXPERIENCE OF THE HOST COUNTRIES. New York: Praeger Publishers, 1970. 432 p.

A collection of essays on the role of foreign investment in the following countries: Argentina, Australia, Belgium, Canada, France, India, Japan, Norway, South Africa, Spain, Tunisia, the United Kingdom, and Yugoslavia.

Longrigg, Stephen H. OIL IN THE MIDDLE EAST. 3d ed. New York:

Oxford University Press, 1968. xiii, 305 p.

> One of the most complete studies of the evolution of the oil in-
> dustry in the Middle East.

McCreary, Edward A. THE AMERICANIZATION OF EUROPE; THE IMPACT
OF AMERICANS AND AMERICAN BUSINESS ON THE UNCOMMON MARKET.
Garden City, N.Y.: Doubleday, 1964. 295 p.

Model, Leo. "The Politics of Private Foreign Investment." FOREIGN AF-
FAIRS 45 (June 1967): 639-51.

> Discusses how and why U.S. foreign companies need to adapt to
> the changing political climate of host countries.

Moran, Theodore H. "Foreign Expansion as an 'Institutional Necessity' for
U.S. Corporate Capitalism: The Search for a Radical Model." WORLD POLI-
TICS 25 (April 1973): 369-86.

> Discounting the foreign investment models of surplus capital and
> declining profits, Moran argues that foreign investment is an insti-
> tutional necessity for the large, diversified multinational firm.
> Such firms do not expand in foreign countries because of high
> profits alone, but rather because of their desire for controlling
> markets. The expansion of American corporate business is best
> explained by the "product cycle" model, which views foreign ex-
> pansion as a necessary corollary of American capitalism.

_____. "New Deal or Raw Deal in Raw Materials." FOREIGN POLICY 5
(Winter 1971-72): 119-36.

> Suggests that nationalization of raw-materials industries may be
> politically advantageous but that there are certain hidden eco-
> nomic costs that may result in lower total earnings.

_____. "Transnational Strategies of Protection and Defense by Multinational
Corporations: Spreading the Risk and Raising the Cost for Nationalization in
Natural Resources." INTERNATIONAL ORGANIZATION 27 (Spring 1973):
273-87.

> A case study of how cooperative transnational policies pay long-
> term dividends. The study examines the role of the Kennecott and
> Anaconda copper companies in Chile and suggests that the "trans-
> national" strategy pursued by Kennecott resulted in economic bene-
> fits to the firm at a time of great political risk.

Nehrt, Lee C. THE POLITICAL CLIMATE FOR FOREIGN INVESTMENT.
New York: Praeger Publishers, 1970. 424 p.

> Nehrt presents an analytical framework for evaluating the political
> climate for foreign investment and then applies the model to

Algeria, Morocco, and Tunisia.

Odell, Peter R.   OIL AND WORLD POWER: BACKGROUND TO THE OIL CRISIS. Harmondsworth, Engl.: Penguin Books, 1974. 245 p.

A concise, readable account of the economics and politics of oil. The study examines the production and consumption of oil and the role of firms and governments of both producing and consuming nations. Chapters 8 and 9 deal with the domestic and international political dimensions of oil.

Oliver, Covey T.   "The Andean Foreign Investment Code: A New Phase in the Quest for Normative Order as to Direct Foreign Investment." AMERICAN JOURNAL OF INTERNATIONAL LAW 66 (October 1972): 763-84.

Ozaki, Robert S.   THE CONTROL OF IMPORTS AND FOREIGN CAPITAL IN JAPAN. New York: Praeger Publishers, 1972. xvii, 309 p.

A case study of Japan's postwar efforts to control the entry of foreign capital and imports.

Ray, Dennis M.   "Corporations and American Foreign Relations." THE ANNALS OF THE AMERICAN ACADEMY OF POLITICAL AND SOCIAL SCIENCE 403 (September 1972): 80-92.

Corporations influence the foreign policy-making process not only by the objectives they pursue but also by their institutional power. The institutional "bias" of business is transferred to government through business executives who leave their corporate posts to serve in top government positions.

Robinson, Richard D.   INTERNATIONAL BUSINESS POLICY. New York: Holt, Rinehart and Winston, 1964. 252 p.

A general study of the policies, problems, and issues involved in direct foreign investment.

Rogers, William D.   "United States Investment in Latin America: A Critical Appraisal." VIRGINIA JOURNAL OF INTERNATIONAL LAW 11 (March 1971): 246-55.

After reviewing some of the important problems of U.S. investment in Latin America, Rogers offers a number of suggestions to U.S. companies and host countries that will promote good relations between them.

Root, Franklin R.   "U.S. Business Abroad and the Political Risks." MSU BUSINESS TOPICS 16 (Winter 1968): 73-80.

Rubin, Seymour J.   "The International Firm and the National Jurisdiction."
In THE INTERNATIONAL CORPORATION, edited by Charles P. Kindleberger,
pp. 179-204. Cambridge, Mass.: M.I.T. Press, 1970.

_____. "Nationalization and Private Foreign Investment: The Role of Govern-
ment." WORLD POLITICS 2 (July 1950): 482-510.

Salera, Virgil. "Liquidate U.S. Direct Investments?" INTER-AMERICAN
ECONOMIC AFFAIRS 24 (Summer 1970): 31-39.

   Attempts to refute Hirschman's thesis that both the United States
   and Latin America benefit by partial liquidation of direct foreign
   investments.

Schmitt, Hans O. "Foreign Capital and Social Conflict in Indonesia, 1950-
1958." ECONOMIC DEVELOPMENT AND CULTURAL CHANGE 10 (April
1962): 284-92.

   A study of the relationship between Dutch foreign investments and
   the political and economic climate in Indonesia.

Servan-Schreiber, J.J. THE AMERICAN CHALLENGE. Translated from the
French by Ronald Steel. New York: Atheneum Publishers, 1968. 278 p.

   A popular and well-known account of the challenge of the United
   States to Western European economic independence. Servan-
   Schreiber attributes the increasing influence of U.S. business on
   the European continent to the organizational and managerial skills
   of the Americans and suggests that if Europe is to maintain its
   economic independence it must bring about internal political, social, and economic reforms.

Shwadran, Benjamin. THE MIDDLE EAST, OIL AND THE GREAT POWERS.
2d ed. New York: Council for Middle Eastern Affairs Press, 1959. 529 p.

   A study of the domestic and international political tensions and
   conflicts involved in the development of the oil industry in the
   Middle East. Shwadran shows how the major oil companies strug-
   gled among themselves and with host governments to stake out
   economic spheres of production.

Smith, Richard Austin. "Nationalism Threatens U.S. Investment." FORTUNE
72 (August 1965): 126-31.

   An examination of the French, German, and Italian positions on
   U.S. foreign investment in their countries.

Tanzer, Michael. THE POLITICAL ECONOMY OF INTERNATIONAL OIL
AND THE UNDERDEVELOPED COUNTRIES. Boston: Beacon Press, 1969.
435 p.

Written before the oil-producing countries established a successful cartel, this study discounts the power and influence of the oil-producing states and suggests that the real determinants of the political economy of oil are the large international oil companies. In addition to case studies of oil production and consumption in selected developing countries, Tanzer examines the role of various forces on the political economy of oil, including host and parent governments, international organizations, and the Soviet Union.

Vernon, Raymond. "Foreign Enterprises and Developing Nations in the Raw Materials Industries." AMERICAN ECONOMIC REVIEW 60 (May 1970): 122-26.

Discusses the major sources of tension between foreign industries and host countries in the production of primary commodities, including oil, copper, and aluminum.

_____. "Foreign-Owned Enterprise in the Developing Countries." PUBLIC POLICY 15 (1966): 361-80.

An examination of some of the basic issues on foreign investment in the LDCs. Vernon suggests that such investment has had important benefits but that these cannot be measured carefully. The indeterminant nature of foreign investment thus does not alleviate the political concerns of the LDCs.

_____, ed. BIG BUSINESS AND THE STATE; CHANGING RELATIONS IN WEST EUROPE. Cambridge, Mass.: Harvard University Press, 1974. 310 p.

_____. HOW LATIN AMERICA VIEWS THE U.S. INVESTOR. New York: Praeger Publishers, 1966. 117 p.

Four excellent essays, one by Vernon himself, on Latin American attitudes toward U.S. direct investment.

Whitman, Marina von Neumann. GOVERNMENT RISK-SHARING IN FOREIGN INVESTMENT. Princeton, N.J.: Princeton University Press, 1965. 358 p.

A study of six major American and international institutions involved in sharing foreign business risks. The author suggests that the six agencies--the Agency for International Development, the Export-Import Bank, the Investment Guaranty Program, the World Bank, the International Finance Corporation, and the Inter-American Development Bank--have played an important role in encouraging long-term capital movements.

_____. THE UNITED STATES INVESTMENT GUARANTY PROGRAM AND PRIVATE FOREIGN INVESTMENT. Princeton Studies in International Finance, no. 9. Princeton, N.J.: International Finance Section, Department of Economics, Princeton University, 1959. 91 p.

> A historical and analytical study of how the U.S. government has tried to encourage and protect direct foreign investment in the LDCs.

Wilkins, Mira. THE MATURING OF MULTINATIONAL ENTERPRISE: AMERICAN BUSINESS ABROAD FROM 1914 TO 1970. Cambridge, Mass.: Harvard University Press, 1974. xvi, 590 p.

> An exhaustive historical account of the twentieth-century development of U.S. foreign investment.

Yanaga, Chitoshi. BIG BUSINESS IN JAPANESE POLITICS. New Haven, Conn.: Yale University Press, 1968. 371 p.

> Analyzes the impact of Japanese business pressure groups on the development of domestic and foreign policies.

B. THE MULTINATIONAL CORPORATION

Adelman, M.A. "The Multinational Corporation in World Petroleum." In THE INTERNATIONAL CORPORATION, edited by Charles P. Kindleberger, pp. 227-42. Cambridge, Mass.: M.I.T. Press, 1970.

> Argues that all major groups interested in oil--host governments, the oil companies, and the governments of the consuming countries--want higher oil prices but for different reasons.

Ajami, Fuad. "Corporate Giants: Some Global Social Costs." INTERNATIONAL STUDIES QUARTERLY 16 (December 1972): 511-29.

Alger, Chadwick F. "The Multinational Corporation and the Future of the International System." ANNALS OF THE AMERICAN ACADEMY OF POLITICAL AND SOCIAL SCIENCE 403 (September 1972): 104-15.

> The multinational corporation is encouraging the bipolarization of the international system into rich and poor regions. Unless this process is checked, the tensions and conflicts could increase in the world. MNCs, along with nongovernmental organizations and intergovernmental agencies, must respond to the interests and needs of the poor states.

Barnet, Richard J., and Mueller, Ronald E. GLOBAL REACH: THE POWER OF THE MULTINATIONAL CORPORATIONS. New York: Simon & Schuster, 1974. 478 p.

> In this popular and widely read study, Barnet and Mueller deplore the increasing influence of MNCs because of their detrimental social and economic effects in the LDCs. The authors suggest

that the behavior of international corporations should be regulated internationally.

Behrman, Jack N. "Multinational Corporations, Transnational Interests, and National Sovereignty." COLUMBIA JOURNAL OF WORLD BUSINESS 4 (March–April 1966): 15–21.

A discussion of the nature and dimensions of political tensions between MNCs and host and parent countries.

_____. "The Multinational Enterprise: Its Initiatives and Governmental Re-actions." JOURNAL OF INTERNATIONAL LAW AND ECONOMICS 6 (January 1972): 215–34.

An analysis of the nature and influence of the MNC on the international system. Behrman reviews U.S. policy toward global firms.

_____. NATIONAL INTERESTS AND THE MULTINATIONAL ENTERPRISE: TENSIONS AMONG THE NORTH ATLANTIC COUNTRIES. Englewood Cliffs, N.J.: Prentice-Hall, 1970. 194 p.

Despite the economic contributions of MNCs to host countries, large business enterprises constitute a major challenge to the sovereignty of the host states. If tensions are to be eased between foreign firms and host governments, some regulations governing MNCs must be implemented.

Chandler, Geoffrey. "The Myth of Oil Power: International Groups and National Sovereignty." INTERNATIONAL AFFAIRS 46 (October 1970): 710–18.

The popular view that MNCs, particularly oil extractive industries, are diminishing the sovereignty of states is a myth. Foreign companies are subject to the laws and power of host governments, which can tax, nationalize, and influence their behavior to suit national objectives.

Diebold, John. "Why Be Scared of Them?" FOREIGN POLICY 12 (Fall 1973): 79–95.

Argues that MNCs can help improve the level of economic development in the LDCs. If friction is to be avoided between firms and governments, however, specific international policy guidelines should be developed.

Dunning, John H., ed. THE MULTINATIONAL ENTERPRISE. New York: Praeger Publishers, 1971. 368 p.

These papers, prepared for a multinational enterprise conference in Reading, England, focus on the nature of the relationship between firms and host nations and on the problem of distributing economic benefits generated by foreign enterprise.

Duren, Albrecht. "Multinational Companies as a Political Problem." WORLD TODAY 28 (November 1972): 473-82.

Despite the growing political opposition to MNCs in the developing countries, Duren is optimistic that the countervailing power of international labor groups can help to ease some of the negative attitudes toward foreign investment.

Evan, Harry Z. "The Multinational Oil Company and the Nation-State." JOURNAL OF WORLD TRADE LAW 4 (1970): 666-85.

A discussion of the political and economic dynamics among four major actors of the oil industry--the oil companies, the parent governments, the host governments, and the governments of oil-consuming nations.

Evans, Peter B. "National Autonomy and Economic Development: Critical Perspectives on Multinational Corporations in Poor Countries." In TRANS-NATIONAL RELATIONS AND WORLD POLITICS, edited by Robert O. Keohane and Joseph S. Nye, Jr., pp. 325-42. Cambridge, Mass.: Harvard University Press, 1972.

Sketches some of the consequences of the poor states' increased autonomy from the rich industrial countries. Although Evans agrees that there are certain benefits from increased separation, there are also some negative consequences. National autonomy will not provide ready-made solutions to the problems of the LDCs; rather, it will provide a new framework in which to seek solutions.

Fells, Richard. GLOBAL CORPORATIONS; THE EMERGING SYSTEM OF WORLD ECONOMIC POWER. New York: Interbook, 1972. 242 p.

Examines the objectives, processes, and strategies of global firms.

Gabriel, Peter. "MNCs in the Third World: Is Conflict Unavoidable?" HARVARD BUSINESS REVIEW 50 (July-August 1972): 92-102.

If conflict between MNCs and the governments of the LDCs is to be avoided, both parties must be willing to compromise. The basic requirements for a "denouement based on mutual accomodation" are the lowering of business risks in the LDCs and strict compliance with government-MNC contracts.

Hartshorn, J.E. POLITICS AND WORLD OIL ECONOMICS: AN ACCOUNT OF THE INTERNATIONAL OIL INDUSTRY IN ITS POLITICAL ENVIRONMENT. Rev. ed. New York: Praeger Publishers, 1967. 404 p.

For annotation, see section A, this chapter.

Heilbroner, Robert L. "The Multinational Corporation and the Nation-State." NEW YORK REVIEW OF BOOKS, 11 February 1971, pp. 20-25.

> Heilbroner argues that both nation-states and MNCs are inadequate instruments for organizing human societies, and that they should be replaced by a new system of world order. The discussion of MNCs is based on an excellent analytical survey of recent literature on the subject.

Hodges, Michael. MULTINATIONAL CORPORATIONS AND NATIONAL GOVERNMENT: A CASE STUDY OF THE UNITED KINGDOM'S EXPERIENCE, 1964-70. Farnborough, Engl.: Sage House; Lexington Mass.: Lexington Books, 1974. 300 p.

> A study of the British Labor Government's policy toward the MNC during the 1964-70 period. Hodges found that during this time the MNC was not of major concern to British political leaders. Chapter 1 provides a useful analysis of the interrelationship of foreign investment and domestic politics.

Howe, Martyn. "Resistance to the Multinational Corporation." WORLD AFFAIRS 132 (September 1969): 146-59.

Hymer, Stephen. "The Multinational Corporation and the Law of Uneven Development." In ECONOMICS AND WORLD ORDER: FROM THE 1970'S TO THE 1990'S, edited by Jagdish N. Bhagwati, pp. 113-40. New York: World Law Fund, 1972.

> The natural consequence of private enterprise is uneven development, that is, development and underdevelopment, poverty and wealth. The large, powerful MNC is a part of this process, and as it spreads its influence in the world it will tend to spread economic benefits unevenly. Hymer suggests that the negative effects of MNCs should be controlled through regional planning.

Ingram, George M. "The International Corporation: A New Challenge to the Discipline." S.A.I.S. REVIEW 14 (Spring 1970): 3-11.

> Examining relations between MNCs and host governments, Ingram probes the major issues that need to be further explored by political scientists.

Keohane, Robert O., and Ooms, Van Doorn. "The Multinational Enterprise and World Political Economy." INTERNATIONAL ORGANIZATION 26 (Winter 1972): 84-120.

> A critical analysis of eleven articles on the MNC.

_____. "The Multinational Firm and International Regulation." INTERNA-
TIONAL ORGANIZATION 29 (Winter 1975): 170-209.

> The authors examine some of the political and economic effects of
> foreign investment, review some of the methods of promoting such
> investment, and discuss possible policies and strategies for regulat-
> ing the MNC.

Kindleberger, Charles P., ed. THE INTERNATIONAL CORPORATION; A
SYMPOSIUM. Cambridge, Mass.: M.I.T. Press, 1970. vii, 415 p.

> The papers, prepared for a seminar on the international corpora-
> tion, examine different aspects of the MNC, including theoretical,
> financial, technological, legal, and political dimensions.

Krause, Lawrence B. "The International Economic System and the Multinational Corporation." ANNALS OF THE AMERICAN ACADEMY OF POLITICAL
AND SOCIAL SCIENCE 403 (September 1972): 93-103.

> The MNC is encouraging the integration of the world economy
> but it is placing major stress on the present international monetary
> system. New policies are needed to ensure a competitive world
> market.

Krause, Walter. "The Implications of UNCTAD III for Multinational Enterprise."
JOURNAL OF INTER-AMERICAN STUDIES AND WORLD AFFAIRS 15 (February
1973): 46-59.

Leyton-Brown, David. "The Multinational Enterprise and Conflict in Canadian-
American Relations." INTERNATIONAL ORGANIZATION 28 (Autumn 1974):
733-54.

Litvak, Isaiah A., and Maule, Christopher J. "Foreign Corporate Social Re-
sponsibility in Less Developed Economies." JOURNAL OF WORLD TRADE
LAW 9 (March-April 1975): 121-35.

> The authors review the operations of two foreign companies in
> Guayana in order to develop a series of policy implications for
> allowing corporate profitability with maximum acceptance to host
> countries.

Lodge, George C. "Make Progress the Product." FOREIGN POLICY 12
(Fall 1973): 96-107.

> The principal problem of MNCs is to reconcile their interests with
> those of host countries. To do this, both corporations and host
> countries must have a clear set of priorities. There are four things
> MNCs should do to promote long-term stable relations with host
> nations: identify the most reliable political order, help LDCs de-
> fine their interests, define the companies' objectives, and attempt
> to work out a mutually advantageous investment program.

Longrigg, Stephen H. OIL IN THE MIDDLE EAST. 3d ed. New York: Oxford University Press, 1968. xiii, 305 p.

One of the most complete studies of the evolution of the oil industry in the Middle East.

Miles, Caroline M. "The International Corporation." INTERNATIONAL AFFAIRS 45 (April 1969): 259-60.

Discusses why the MNC has become a more important political and economic subject in international relations.

Miller, Arthur S. "The Global Corporation and American Constitutionalism: Some Political Consequences of Economic Power." JOURNAL OF INTERNATIONAL LAW AND ECONOMICS 6 (January 1972): 235-46.

Discusses some reasons why the nation-state has declined in influence. One of the principal forces working against the established political order of states is the global corporation, which is itself a political entity.

_____. "The Multinational Corporation and the Nation State." JOURNAL OF WORLD TRADE LAW 7 (May-June 1973): 267-92.

The MNC has had three important consequences for the state: it has eroded the state's sovereignty; it has encouraged the concept of corporate citizenship; and it has increased the level of interdependence between firms and states. The implication of these changes on American constitutionalism is briefly examined.

Mueller, Ronald E. "Poverty is the Product." FOREIGN POLICY 13 (Winter 1973-74): 71-102.

Examines the effect of MNCs on the LDCs and finds that the technological contribution of firms is exaggerated, that firms are a financial drain instead of a net gain, and that the balance of payments effect of foreign corporations is no better than those of local firms. The MNC will continue to impoverish the poorest segment of Third World nations.

Nye, Joseph S., Jr. "Multinational Enterprise and Prospects for Regional and Global Political Integration." ANNALS OF THE AMERICAN ACADEMY OF POLITICAL AND SOCIAL SCIENCE 403 (September 1972): 116-38.

Although the MNC is a potentially important force for regional integration, global firms may weaken integration by decreasing regional and global identity and by increasing inequality. Whether integration is encouraged by MNCs must be determined on a case-by-case basis.

Osterberg, D., and Ajami, Fuad. "The Multinational Corporation: Expanding the Frontiers of World Politics." JOURNAL OF CONFLICT RESOLUTION 15 (1971): 457-70.

> A general analysis of the increasing role of the MNC in international relations. Some negative consequences of global firms are discussed.

Pinelo, Adalberto J. THE MULTINATIONAL CORPORATION AS A FORCE IN LATIN AMERICAN POLITICS: A CASE STUDY OF THE INTERNATIONAL PETROLEUM COMPANY IN PERU. New York: Praeger Publishers, 1973. 171 p.

> A useful case study of how a large foreign corporation operates in a relatively poor, backward state.

Robinson, Richard D. "The Developing Countries, Development, and the Multinational Corporation." ANNALS OF THE AMERICAN ACADEMY OF POLITICAL AND SOCIAL SCIENCE 403 (September 1972): 67-79.

> Given the political tensions aroused by foreign corporations in the LDCs, Robinson suggests two approaches to investment: (1) the development of transnational firms which are owned and managed multinationally; and (2) the development of a transnational association of corporations.

Rolfe, Sidney E. THE MULTINATIONAL CORPORATION. New York: Foreign Policy Association, 1970. 62 p.

> Discusses some of the major political and economic consequences of the MNC on host countries and the world economy.

Rolfe, Sidney E., and Damm, Walter, eds. THE MULTINATIONAL CORPORATION IN THE WORLD ECONOMY: DIRECT INVESTMENT IN PERSPECTIVE. New York: Praeger Publishers, 1970. 169 p.

> A collection of papers on MNCs given at an international conference in Washington, D.C. The studies focus on the international political economy of global firms.

Said, Abdul A., and Simmons, Luis R., eds. THE NEW SOVEREIGNS; MULTINATIONAL CORPORATIONS AS WORLD POWERS. Englewood Cliffs, N.J.: Prentice-Hall, 1975. vi, 186 p.

> An excellent anthology of studies on the political, technical, sociological, and economic aspects of the MNC. Particularly helpful are the following chapters: James R. Kurth, "The Multinational Corporation, U.S. Foreign Policy, and the Less Developed Countries"; and Theodore A. Couloumbis and Elias P. Georgiades, "The Impact of the Multinational Corporation on the International System."

Shaker, Frank. "The Multinational Corporation: The New Imperialism."
COLUMBIA JOURNAL OF WORLD BUSINESS 5 (November 1970): 80–84.

> United States companies have been assaulting the cultures and
> economies of the LDCs, and if American MNCs are to be ac-
> cepted in foreign countries in the future, they will have to elim-
> inate their exploitative image.

Stephenson, Hugh. THE COMING CLASH: THE IMPACT OF MULTINATIONAL
CORPORATIONS ON THE NATION STATE. London: Weidenfeld and Nicol-
son, 1972. 189 p.

> A general impressionistic account of the impact of the MNC on
> the nation-state.

Tannenbaum, Frank. "The Survival of the Fittest." COLUMBIA JOURNAL
OF WORLD BUSINESS 3 (March–April 1968): 13–20.

> Tannenbaum suggests that the MNC may supplant the nation-state
> as the principal political unit in the world. The writer expresses
> the hope for a new world order in which the nation-state is re-
> placed by an international corporation responsible for governing
> the world.

Turner, Louis. MULTINATIONAL COMPANIES AND THE THIRD WORLD.
New York: Hill & Wang, 1973. ix, 294 p.

> Turner, a sociologist, examines the nature and dynamics of the
> relations between MNCs and host governments in the LDCs.

Vernon, Raymond. "Does Society Also Profit?" FOREIGN POLICY 13 (Winter 1973–74): 103–17.

> The MNC brings about both beneficial and detrimental consequences
> in LDCs. "But multinational enterprises are neither cops nor rob-
> bers, good guys nor bad guys."

_____. "Multinational Business and National Economic Goals." In TRANS-
NATIONAL RELATIONS AND WORLD POLITICS, edited by Robert O. Keohane
and Joseph S. Nye, Jr., pp. 343–55. Cambridge, Mass.: Harvard University
Press, 1972.

> Increased economic interdependence from MNCs has resulted in
> improved efficiency in the world economy but it poses a challenge
> to the sovereignty of states. To cope more effectively with the
> new interdependent system, states should improve their coordina-
> tion of economic policies.

_____. MULTINATIONAL ENTERPRISE AND NATIONAL SECURITY. Adelphi
Papers, no. 74. London: Institute for Strategic Studies, 1971. 34 p.

Because MNCs will become increasingly more independent of parent states, foreign subsidiaries will tend to be less associated with foreign policy concerns of their home states.

_____. "Multinational Enterprise and National Sovereignty." HARVARD LAW REVIEW 45 (March–April 1967): 156–72.

Discusses some possible future political and economic tensions between MNCs and host governments and suggests how some of the tensions could be eased.

_____. SOVEREIGNTY AT BAY: THE MULTINATIONAL SPREAD OF U.S. ENTERPRISES. New York: Basic Books, 1971. 326 p.

This study, a product of a large-scale project on the MNC by the Harvard University Business School, examines the growth of global firms and the increasingly important political and economic role they play in the international system. Vernon examines the relationships of companies to host countries, discussing in particular the problems posed by balance of payments, competing ideologies, and differing cultures. An excellent source of data on U.S. raw materials and manufacturing firms.

_____, ed. THE ECONOMIC AND POLITICAL CONSEQUENCES OF MULTINATIONAL ENTERPRISE: AN ANTHOLOGY. Boston: Division of Research, Graduate School of Business Administration, Harvard University, 1972. 236 p.

A collection of articles on the multinational firm, written by the author from 1968 to 1971. Most of the materials are developed in his study SOVEREIGNTY AT BAY (see above).

Von Lazar, Arpad. "Multinational Enterprises and Latin American Integration, A Sociopolitical View." JOURNAL OF INTER-AMERICAN STUDIES 11 (January 1969): 111–28.

Through the use of interviews, the author seeks to evaluate the possible impact of MNCs on Latin American political integration.

Wallace, Don, Jr., ed. INTERNATIONAL CONTROL OF INVESTMENT: THE DUSSELDORF CONFERENCE ON MULTINATIONAL CORPORATIONS. Published in cooperation with the Institute for International and Foreign Trade Law, Georgetown University Law Center. New York: Praeger Publishers, 1974. 281 p.

A compilation of papers and proceedings of a conference on the desirability and feasibility of establishing an international organization which might help regulate MNCs. The general consensus of the participants was that the problems posed by the MNC in the LDCs can best be handled without the establishment of a new organization, although some cooperative action might be desirable.

Wells, Louis T., Jr. "The Multinational Business Enterprise: What Kind of International Organization?" INTERNATIONAL ORGANIZATION 25 (Summer 1971): 447-64.

Discusses some of the common political and economic characteristics of MNCs.

Zink, Dolph Warren. THE POLITICAL RISKS FOR MULTINATIONAL ENTERPRISE IN DEVELOPING COUNTRIES: WITH A CASE STUDY OF PERU. New York: Praeger Publishers, 1973. xix, 185 p.

In the first part of this volume Zink presents a framework for measuring potential political risks and for developing appropriate business policies. In the second part he uses the framework to measure and evaluate foreign investment practices in Peru.

Chapter 8

IMPERIALISM

Imperialism is the theory and practice by which one state seeks to expand its influence and control over other states. The subject of imperialism relates closely to economics and foreign policy because one of the popular explanations of this phenomenon is the Marxist theory, which holds that the chief motivation for international expansion and dominance is the maximization of national economic interests. In this chapter we therefore examine the significant information sources relating to both the theory (part one) and practice (part two) of imperialism. The third part of this chapter examines the literature on the economic causes of war, a corollary theme of imperialism. Given the popularity of the Marxist notion of imperialism, it is not surprising that the economic interpretation of international conflict has also received widespread attention.

A. THEORIES OF IMPERIALISM

Ackermann, Frank, and Kindleberger, Charles P. "Magdoff on Imperialism: Two Views." PUBLIC POLICY 11 (Summer 1961): 525-31.

> A critical analysis of Harry Magdoff's THE AGE OF IMPERIALISM: THE ECONOMICS OF U.S. FOREIGN POLICY (see section B) from two different perspectives. Ackermann praises Magdoff's book, while Kindleberger finds the study's thesis weak and inadequate.

Amin, Samir. ACCUMULATION ON A WORLD SCALE: A CRITIQUE OF THE THEORY OF UNDERDEVELOPMENT. 2 vols. New York: Monthly Review Press, 1974. 666 p.

> Amin argues that economic imperialism has infected not only the center (capitalist nations), but the periphery (LDCs) as well. Within each peripheral country there is a center which applies imperialism domestically. Underdevelopment is fostered by the backward nations themselves, which are linked to global imperialism through the international center-periphery structure.

Blaug, Mark. "Economic Imperialism Revisited." YALE REVIEW 50 (March 1961): 335-49.

Boulding, Kenneth E., and Mukerjee, Tapan, eds. ECONOMIC IMPERIALISM; A BOOK OF READINGS. Ann Arbor: University of Michigan Press, 1972. xviii, 338 p.

> A collection of important theoretical essays and case studies on imperialism. Because the materials focus on both the meaning of the concept and the empirical validity of the theory, the readings are one of the best contemporary introductions to the subject. A lengthy bibliography is included.

Bukharin, Nikolai I. IMPERIALISM AND THE ACCUMULATION OF CAPITAL. Translated by Rudolf Wickmann. 1926. Reprint. New York: Monthly Review Press, 1972. 270 p.

> A significant early twentieth-century Marxist study of the tendency of capital to concentrate under a capitalist system. The study is based on a critical evaluation of Rosa Luxemburg's earlier works on the subject (see below, this section).

_____. IMPERIALISM AND WORLD ECONOMY. New York: International Publishers, 1929. 173 p.

> This classic Marxist study of imperialism is significant because it attempts to refine and establish the empirical validity of Lenin's earlier study on the subject. Bukharin examines the nature of the world economy and attempts to show why imperialism follows of necessity from capitalist economic structures. The Marxist notion that capitalism will ultimately collapse is reiterated.

Cohen, Benjamin J. THE QUESTION OF IMPERIALISM: THE POLITICAL ECONOMY OF DOMINANCE AND DEPENDENCE. New York: Basic Books, 1973. 280 p.

> The Marxist and radical theories of imperialism are invalid both logically and empirically: At the level of logic they are invalid because it is impossible to prove that economic imperialism is a necessary result of capitalism or that poor countries are necessarily exploited; and they are invalid at the empirical level because the LDCs have rarely played the role ascribed to them, either as markets, investment outlets, or sources of raw materials. "The gains of international capitalist economy do not necessarily go to the rich." According to Cohen, the major explanation for imperialism is power politics, for a nation can find security in the international system only as it pursues its own interests.

Deutsch, Karl W. "Theories of Imperialism and Neocolonialism." In TESTING THEORIES OF ECONOMIC IMPERIALISM, edited by Steven J. Rosen and James R. Kurth, pp. 15-33. Lexington, Mass.: Lexington Books, 1974.

> An analysis of the following theories of imperialism: "folk," conservative, liberal, Marxist, sociological and psychological, and dependencia.

Dos Santos, Theotonio. "The Structure of Dependence." AMERICAN ECO-
NOMIC REVIEW: PAPERS AND PROCEEDINGS 60 (May 1970): 231-36.

> Attempts to demonstrate that the Latin American economic depen-
> dence on the developed countries cannot be overcome without a
> fundamental change in internal structures and external relations.

Emmanuel, Arghiri. UNEQUAL EXCHANGE: A STUDY OF THE IMPERIALISM
OF TRADE. New York: Monthly Review Press, 1972. xiii, 453 p.

> The world capitalist economy distributes gains from trade unequally.
> It is the imperialism of trade that is responsible for the develop-
> ment of underdevelopment in the world.

Fann, K.T., and Hodges, Donald C., eds. READINGS IN U.S. IMPERIALISM.
Boston: Porter Sargent Publisher, An Extending Horizons Book, 1971. 394 p.

> A collection of essays on economic imperialism by contemporary
> Marxist writers.

Fieldhouse, David K., ed. THE THEORY OF CAPITALIST IMPERIALISM. London: Longmans, Green and Co., 1967. xix, 202 p.

> A collection of useful readings on the Lenin-Hobson theory of
> imperialism, focusing on its foundations, application, and evalua-
> tion.

Galtung, Johan. "A Structural Theory of Imperialism." JOURNAL OF PEACE
RESEARCH 8 (1971): 81-118.

> According to Galtung's theory, the world is divided into countries
> located at the center and periphery, with each nation having a
> center and peripheral region itself. The gains from trade move
> from the periphery to the center, both within countries as well as
> between states. Unlike the system in Lenin's theory, this system
> is self-perpetuating.

Hammond, Richard. "Imperialism: Sidelights on a Stereotype." THE JOUR-
NAL OF ECONOMIC HISTORY 21 (December 1961): 582-96.

Heimann, Eduard. "Schumpeter and the Problems of Imperialism." SOCIAL
RESEARCH 19 (June 1952): 177-97.

Hobson, J.A. IMPERIALISM, A STUDY. 1902. Reprint. London: George
Allen & Unwin, 1948. 379 p.

> Unquestionably one of the most influential studies of economic
> imperialism, to a large extent because Lenin's classic study on
> imperialism builds on this work. Although not a Marxist, Hobson

argues that the principal force behind imperialism is capitalism--a
system that produces too much but consumes too little. The capitalist system must therefore solve the domestic imbalance in the
international system.

Hovde, Bryniolf J. "Socialist Theories of Imperialism Prior to the Great War."
JOURNAL OF POLITICAL ECONOMY 36 (October 1928): 569-691.

Koebner, Richard. "The Concept of Economic Imperialism." ECONOMIC
HISTORY REVIEW, 2d ser., 2 (1949): 1-29.

Koebner, Richard, and Schmidt, Helmut D. IMPERIALISM: THE STORY AND
SIGNIFICANCE OF A POLITICAL WORD, 1840-1960. New York: Cambridge
University Press, 1964. 432 p.

> An exhaustive study of the use of the term "imperialism" from the
> early nineteenth century through the mid-twentieth century. A
> useful guide to the subject.

Landes, David S. "Some Thoughts on the Nature of Economic Imperialism."
JOURNAL OF ECONOMIC HISTORY 21 (December 1961): 496-521.

> Imperialism occurs because of the disparity of power in the world.
> Politics, not economics, explains the practice of imperialism.

Langer, William L. "A Critique of Imperialism." FOREIGN AFFAIRS 35
(October 1935): 102-19.

Lenin, Vladimir I. IMPERIALISM: THE HIGHEST STAGE OF CAPITALISM.
1917. Reprint. New York: International Publishers Co., 1972. 127 p.

> One of Lenin's most significant works and certainly one of the
> most influential studies on imperialism. Building on the work of
> J.A. Hobson, Lenin argues that capitalist states must inevitably
> pursue imperialism in order to survive. The need to dominate
> other states in the international system is based on the need to
> gain new markets and obtain more raw materials.

Lichtheim, George. IMPERIALISM. New York: Praeger Publishers, 1971.
183 p.

> Lichtheim, a democratic Socialist, traces the historical and theo-
> retical basis of imperialism in order to develop a more precise
> conceptual understanding of its operation in the contemporary
> world. The author suggests that a more precise meaning of im-
> perialism may relate more to the postwar political tensions than
> to the domestic economic drives of capitalist states.

Luxemburg, Rosa. THE ACCUMULATION OF CAPITAL. Translated from the

German by Agnes Schwarzschild. 1913. Reprint. New York: Monthly Review Press, 1968. 475 p.

A difficult Marxist economic analysis of the process and implications of capital accumulation under a capitalist system.

_____. THE ACCUMULATION OF CAPITAL--AN ANTI-CRITIQUE. Translated by Rudolf Wichmann. 1923. Reprint. New York: Monthly Review Press, 1972. 140 p.

Written as a sequel to THE ACCUMULATION OF CAPITAL (above), this essay attempts to develop further the Marxist notion that capital concentrates under a capitalist system.

Mack, Andrew. "Comparing Theories of Economic Imperialism." In TESTING THEORIES OF ECONOMIC IMPERIALISM, edited by Steven J. Rosen and James R. Kurth, pp. 35-55. Lexington, Mass.: Lexington Books, 1974.

Compares the classical theory of imperialism with the modern interpretations of Magdoff, Moran, Galtung, and Emmanuel.

_____. "Theories of Imperialism: The European Perspective." JOURNAL OF CONFLICT RESOLUTION 18 (September 1974): 514-35.

A critical analysis of three recent European studies on imperialism: UNEQUAL EXCHANGE: A STUDY OF THE IMPERIALISM OF TRADE by A. Emmanuel; THE EUROPEAN COMMUNITY: A SUPERPOWER IN THE MAKING by Johan Galtung; and STUDIES IN THE THEORY OF IMPERIALISM, edited by R. Owen and R. Sutcliffe.

Magdoff, Harry. "Militarism and Imperialism." AMERICAN ECONOMIC REVIEW: PAPERS AND PROCEEDINGS 60 (May 1970): 237-42.

An ideological discussion of why militarism, imperialism, and capitalism all go together.

Moon, Parker Thomas. IMPERIALISM AND WORLD POLITICS. New York: Macmillan Co., 1926. 583 p.

A balanced historical and analytical discussion of nineteenth- and early twentieth-century imperialism. The volume became one of the most popular texts on the subject in the 1930s and 1940s.

Moran, Theodore [H.]. "The Theory of International Exploitation in Large Natural Resource Investments." In TESTING THEORIES OF ECONOMIC IMPERIALISM, edited by Steven J. Rosen and James R. Kurth, pp. 163-81. Lexington, Mass.: Lexington Books, 1974.

Moran presents a framework for analyzing foreign firms' relations with host governments, and then applies it to Chile's copper industry. The author argues that the U.S. copper companies were able to exploit Chile's resources because they were able to get domestic political support.

Neisser, Hans. "Economic Imperialism Reconsidered." SOCIAL RESEARCH 27 (Spring 1960): 63-82.

Nkrumah, Kwame. NEO-COLONIALISM: THE LAST STAGE OF IMPERIALISM. New York: International Publishers, 1971. xx, 280 p.

> A neo-imperialist account of direct foreign investment in different sectors of the African economy. The author, the ex-president of Ghana, argues that foreign investment is the contemporary manifestation of imperialism--an imperialism that differs from the nineteenth-century form in that there is economic exploitation without direct political control. The introduction gives a short explanation of the theory of neo-imperialism.

O'Connor, James. "The Meaning of Economic Imperialism." In READINGS IN U.S. IMPERIALISM, edited by K.T. Fann and Donald C. Hodges, pp. 23-68. Boston: Porter Sargent Publisher, An Extending Horizons Book, 1971.

> A short but useful analytical discussion of the Marxist and neo-Marxist views of imperialism.

Rhodes, Robert I., ed. IMPERIALISM AND UNDERDEVELOPMENT: A READER. New York: Monthly Review Press, 1970. 416 p.

> A useful collection of Marxist and neo-Marxist essays on the problem of economic underdevelopment.

Schumpeter, Joseph A. CAPITALISM, SOCIALISM AND DEMOCRACY. 3d ed. New York: Harper & Row, 1950. 425 p.

> A classic comparison of capitalism and socialism with reference to democracy. Chapters 1 to 4 present an insightful critique of Marxism.

_____. IMPERIALISM AND SOCIAL CLASSES. Translated from the German by Heinz Norden. New York: Augustus M. Kelley, 1951. xxv, 221 p.

> The real cause of imperialism is the irrational drives within the leaders of the ruling class, not the capitalist system. Since imperialism is based on the feudal, precapitalist, nonrational conditions of society, and since capitalism tends to eliminate these conditions, "a purely capitalist world can offer no fertile soil to imperialist impulses."

Sherman, Howard. RADICAL POLITICAL ECONOMY; CAPITALISM AND SOCIALISM: A MARXIST-HUMANIST PERSPECTIVE. New York: Basic Books, 1972. xv, 431 p.

A comparative analysis of the capitalist and socialist economic systems.

Sunkel, Osvaldo. "Big Business and 'Dependencia': A Latin America View." FOREIGN AFFAIRS 50 (April 1972): 515-31.

A discussion of some political, social, and economic problems resulting from direct foreign investment in Latin America.

Viner, Jacob. "Finance and Balance of Power Diplomacy." THE SOUTHWESTERN POLITICAL AND SOCIAL SCIENCE QUARTERLY 9 (March 1929): 407-51.

Examines the relationship of international loans of European governments and their balance of power diplomacy from the 1880s until the beginning of the First World War. Viner finds that there is no evidence to support the view that bankers controlled prewar diplomacy, but that instead there is more evidence that "diplomacy exercised a controlling influence over prewar international finance."

Winslow, E.M. "Marxian, Liberal and Sociological Theories of Imperialism." JOURNAL OF POLITICAL ECONOMY 39 (December 1931): 713-58.

A comparative analysis of the common interpretations of imperialism in the early twentieth century. The study focuses on Marxists, selected British and American liberals, and J. Schumpeter.

_____. THE PATTERN OF IMPERIALISM, A STUDY IN THE THEORIES OF POWER. New York: Columbia University Press, 1948. 278 p.

The thesis of this study is that imperialism is primarily a political, not economic, phenomenon.

Wolff, Richard D. "Modern Imperialism: The View from the Metropolis." AMERICAN ECONOMIC REVIEW 60 (May 1970): 225-30.

Argues that MNCs are instruments of imperialism because of their attempt to control raw materials, markets for their goods, and spheres for capital investment. The cooperative efforts of MNCs and their governments result in the control of one economy over the other.

Zeitlin, Irving M. CAPITALISM AND IMPERIALISM: AN INTRODUCTION TO NEO-MARXIAN CONCEPTS. Chicago: Markham Publishing Co., 1972. 128 p.

A short, readable exposition of Marxist and neo-Marxist theory as it relates to capitalism and imperialism. A portion of the study deals with domestic and international economic policies of the United States.

B. THE PRACTICE OF IMPERIALISM

Baran, Paul [A.], and Sweezy, Paul. MONOPOLY CAPITAL: AN ESSAY ON THE AMERICAN ECONOMIC AND SOCIAL ORDER. New York: Monthly Review Press, 1966. 402 p.

Bodenheimer, Susanne. "Dependency and Imperialism: The Roots of Latin American Underdevelopment." In READINGS IN U.S. IMPERIALISM, edited by K.T. Fann and Donald C. Hodges, pp. 155–81. Boston: Porter Sargent Publisher, An Extending Horizons Book, 1971.

> The real explanation for Latin America's economic underdevelopment is imperialism. The "dependency" model of Andre Gunder Frank is helpful in understanding relations between the dominant and dependent states but is unable to focus on the real issue--the relationship of private to public capital in the dominant state.

Brown, Michael B. AFTER IMPERIALISM. 2d ed. London: William Heinemann, 1970. viii, 535 p.

> A sophisticated Marxist study of the theory and practice of imperialism in Great Britain's past and present international economic relations. The last part of the study examines contemporary developments in the international economic system.

Brundenius, Claes. "The Anatomy of Imperialism: Multinational Mining Corporations in Peru." JOURNAL OF PEACE RESEARCH 9 (1972): 189–208.

Frank, Andre Gunder. CAPITALISM AND UNDERDEVELOPMENT IN LATIN AMERICA; HISTORICAL STUDIES OF CHILE AND BRAZIL. New York: Monthly Review Press, 1967. xx, 298 p.

> A Marxist interpretation of Chilean and Brazilian economic history. Frank applies the "dependency" model to these case studies to show that the capitalist system has brought about underdevelopment in both countries.

Goldstein, Walter. "U.S. Economic Penetration of Western Europe." In TESTING THEORIES OF ECONOMIC IMPERIALISM, edited by Steven J. Rosen and James R. Kurth, pp. 211–28. Lexington, Mass.: Lexington Books, 1974.

> Assesses the nature, extent, and impact of U.S. investment in Western Europe. Good source for U.S. foreign investment data.

Grow, Roy F. "Soviet Economic Penetration of China, 1945–1960: 'Imperialism' as a Level of Analysis Problem." In TESTING THEORIES OF ECONOMIC IMPERIALISM, edited by Steven J. Rosen and James R. Kurth, pp. 261–81. Lexington, Mass.: Lexington Books, 1974.

The author, a political scientist, examines the nature of economic relations between China and the Soviet Union during the postwar era. His conclusion is that "the charges of imperialism leveled at the Soviet Union might have some factual basis, depending, of course, on the level of analysis used in ordering the data."

Halliday, Jon, and McCormack, Gavan. JAPANESE IMPERIALISM TODAY. New York: Monthly Review Press, 1973. xviii, 279 p.

A largely descriptive study of the contemporary international economic relations of Japan within a Marxist framework. The study attempts to show that Japan has practiced imperialism with neighboring East Asian states.

Hudson, Michael. SUPER IMPERIALISM: THE ECONOMIC STRATEGY OF AMERICAN EMPIRE. New York: Holt, Rinehart and Winston, 1972. 293 p.

A scholarly, neo-imperialistic analysis of U.S. postwar economic policies, with particular reference to the international monetary system, trade, and aid. Chapters 5 and 6 on U.S. policies toward the World Bank and foreign aid are insightful.

Imlah, Albert H. ECONOMIC ELEMENTS IN THE PAX BRITANNICA; STUDIES IN BRITISH FOREIGN TRADE IN THE NINETEENTH CENTURY. Cambridge, Mass.: Harvard University Press, 1958. 224 p.

Jalee, Pierre. IMPERIALISM IN THE SEVENTIES. Translated by Raymond and Margaret Sokolov. New York: Third Press, 1972. xxvii, 226 p.

Attempts to show the relevancy of Lenin's theory of imperialism to the structure of contemporary Western economic relations.

_____. THE PILLAGE OF THE THIRD WORLD. Translated from the French by Mary Klopper. New York: Monthly Review Press, 1968. 115 p.

A Marxist analysis of contemporary commercial relations between the Third World and the developed industrial states of Western Europe and North America. Jalee argues that the relationship between the LDCs and the rich nations is imperialistic.

Kaufman, Robert R.; Chernotsky, Harry I.; and Geller, Daniel S. "A Preliminary Test of the Theory of Dependency." COMPARATIVE POLITICS 7 (April 1975): 303-30.

Although an attempt is made to measure quantitatively some of the hypotheses of dependency theory, the authors conclude that it is impossible to verify the theory empirically. What is needed is further refinement of the theory and of the techniques necessary to measure it. The writers do suggest, however, that "it would be highly advisable to tone down (or at least reassess) the extravagant claims sometimes made for dependency theory as a framework for understanding all of the problems of Latin American development."

Kay, G.B., ed. POLITICAL ECONOMY OF COLONIALISM IN GHANA. Cambridge: At the University Press, 1972. xvii, 431 p.

A collection of documents on the economic development of Ghana. Kay's introductory chapter traces some of the major issues in the nation's colonial development.

Magdoff, Harry. THE AGE OF IMPERIALISM: THE ECONOMICS OF U.S. FOREIGN POLICY. New York: Monthly Review Press, 1969. 208 p.

Magdoff, a Marxist, argues that the underlying purpose of U.S. economic policy "is nothing less than keeping as much as possible of the world open for trade and investment by the giant multinational corporations." U.S. economic interests have been to keep poor countries dependent through the instrument of foreign investment. For a critical analysis of Magdoff's work, see Ackermann and Kindleberger's "Magdoff on Imperialism: Two Views" (section A, this chapter).

Mandel, Ernest. EUROPE VS. AMERICA--CONTRADICTIONS OF IMPERIALISM. New York: Monthly Review Press, 1970. 160 p.

A Marxist explanation of the contemporary economic tensions between Europe and the United States.

Marer, Paul. "The Political Economy of Soviet Relations with Eastern Europe." In TESTING THEORIES OF ECONOMIC IMPERIALISM, edited by Steven J. Rosen and James R. Kurth, pp. 231-60. Lexington, Mass.: Lexington Books, 1974.

Attempts to measure the extent to which the Soviet Union has exhibited economic imperialism toward Bulgaria, Czechoslovakia, East Germany, Hungary, Poland, and Rumania during the postwar era. Marer found that while the Soviet Union did pursue imperialistic policies from 1945 until the death of Stalin in 1953, there has been little evidence of imperialism since 1953. Indeed, "evidence suggests that the U.S.S.R. might be paying an increasingly steep price for the political benefit it derives from the continued dependence of East European countries on the Soviet Union."

May, Ernest R. AMERICAN IMPERIALISM: A SPECULATIVE ESSAY. New York: Atheneum Publishers, 1968. ix, 239 p.

Odell, John S. "Correlates of U.S. Military Assistance and Military Intervention." In TESTING THEORIES OF ECONOMIC IMPERIALISM, edited by Steven J. Rosen and James R. Kurth, pp. 143-61. Lexington, Mass.: Lexington Books, 1974.

Using quantitative techniques, Odell found that U.S. military intervention was related to military assistance; but, since military involvement was not associated with raw materials or private investment, the validity of the theory of imperialism may be questioned.

Platt, Desmond C.M. FINANCE, TRADE, AND POLITICS IN BRITISH FOREIGN POLICY, 1815–1914. Oxford: Oxford University Press, 1968. xi, 454 p.

Rosen, Steven J. "The Open Door Imperative and U.S. Foreign Policy." In TESTING THEORIES OF ECONOMIC IMPERIALISM, edited by Steven J. Rosen and James R. Kurth, pp. 117–42. Lexington, Mass.: Lexington Books, 1974.

Examines the effect of foreign political disruptions on U.S. trade, oil, and foreign investment. Basing his study on data from five countries (Brazil, Indonesia, Chile, Greece, and Peru), the author finds that political changes do affect the level of foreign American involvement and concern. Specifically, leftward ideological shifts tend to decrease U.S. interest, while righthand shifts tend to increase U.S. economic involvement.

Rosen, Steven J., and Kurth, James R., eds. TESTING THEORIES OF ECONOMIC IMPERIALISM. Lexington, Mass.: Lexington Books, 1974. ix, 284 p.

One of the best collections of contemporary political science research on imperialism. The papers, given at several conferences during 1973, present different theories of imperialism and attempt to measure their validity, largely be examining the behavior of the United States and the Soviet Union. Individual essays are annotated elsewhere in this section.

Semmel, Bernard. THE RISE OF FREE TRADE IMPERIALISM: CLASSICAL POLITICAL ECONOMY, THE EMPIRE OF FREE TRADE AND IMPERIALISM, 1750–1850. Cambridge: At the University Press, 1970. 243 p.

A historical account of the development of Britain's free trade policy during the 1750–1850 period.

Stauffer, Robert B. "The Political Economy of a Coup: Transnational Linkages and Philippine Political Response." JOURNAL OF PEACE RESEARCH 11 (1974): 161–78.

Using Galtung's dependency model, the author examines the political and economic forces that led to the 1972 coup in the Philippines. Stauffer found that there was a harmony of interests between Filipino and American elites, but that there was a disharmony of interests between the elites and the population at large.

Steel, Ronald. PAX AMERICANA. New York: Viking Press, 1967. 371 p.

A polemical treatise on how the United States became a global interventionist power in the postwar era. The shift from isolation to empire, argues Steel, has come about largely by accident and with the best of intentions.

Sternberg, Fritz. "Japan's Economic Imperialism." SOCIAL RESEARCH 12 (September 1945): 328-48.

A discussion of some salient features of Japan's economic policies during the interwar period.

Strachey, John. THE END OF EMPIRE. New York: Random House, 1960. 351 p.

In this study of the development and decay of empires, Strachey argues that the decolonization process has made European powers better off economically, since their resources, energies, and political attention are no longer drained into their former colonies. The study is particularly valuable for those concerned with the breakdown of the colonial system.

Thornton, Archibald P. THE IMPERIAL IDEA AND ITS ENEMIES: A STUDY IN BRITISH POWER. New York: St. Martin's Press, 1959. 370 p.

Tyler, William G., and Wogart, J. Peter. "Economic Dependence and Marginalization: Some Empirical Evidence." JOURNAL OF INTERAMERICAN STUDIES AND WORLD AFFAIRS 15 (February 1973): 36-46.

Viallate, Achille. ECONOMIC IMPERIALISM AND INTERNATIONAL RELATIONS DURING THE LAST FIFTY YEARS. New York: Macmillan Co., 1923. 180 p.

The dominant objective of European powers during the late nineteenth and early twentieth centuries was "economic penetration." The prosperity brought about by economic dependency, however, did not result in economic internationalism but in economic imperialism.

Weaver, James H., ed. MODERN POLITICAL ECONOMY: RADICAL AND ORTHODOX VIEWS ON CRUCIAL ISSUES. Boston: Allyn & Bacon, 1973. 465 p.

In this anthology on domestic and international economic issues two foreign policy questions are examined: "Is the United States an Imperialistic Nation?" and "Is the Vietnam War an Outgrowth of the Political Economic System in the U.S.?" H. Magdoff argues that the United States is an imperialistic state, while B. Cohen sets forth the notion that imperialism is the result of a competitive nation-state system, not the consequence of economic interests. In discussing the second question, L. Keyserling argues that the Vietnam war has had a negative economic impact on the United States, while M. Reich suggests that a high degree of military spending is required to compensate for the lack of demand in the American private sector.

C. THE ECONOMIC CAUSES OF WAR

Aron, Raymond. PEACE AND WAR: A THEORY OF INTERNATIONAL RELA-TIONS. Translated from the French by R. Howard and A. Barker Fox. New York: Praeger Publishers, 1966. 820 p.

In chapter 9 of this monumental study Aron examines the relationship of economics to peace, focusing on four historical perspectives --the mercantilist, the liberal, the Marxist, and the Socialist. Aron argues that there is no necessary connection between economics and foreign policy; war is not an inevitable result of capitalism.

Azar, Edward E. PROBE FOR PEACE: SMALL STATE HOSTILITIES. Minneapolis, Minn.: Burgess Publishing Co., 1973. 89 p.

In the first part of this study Azar examines anthropological, sociological, ecological, socioeconomic, and interaction theories of war.

Barbera, Henry. RICH NATIONS AND POOR IN PEACE AND WAR; CONTINUITY AND CHANGE IN THE DEVELOPMENT HIERARCHY OF SEVENTY NATIONS FROM 1913 THROUGH 1952. Lexington, Mass.: Lexington Books, 1973. 208 p.

A brilliant and well-conceived empirical study of the relationship between war and economic development with a view of determining the impact of the First and Second World Wars on the economies of both rich and poor nations.

Barnet, Richard J. ROOTS OF WAR. Baltimore: Penguin Books, 1973. 350 p.

The reason the United States goes to war is that it is organized for war rather than peace. More specifically, the U.S. tendency to be involved in war is a result of the centralization of power in a national security bureaucracy, the need for continued foreign economic expansion, and the vulnerability of the American people to national security issues. The underlying assumption of this polemical treatise is that war is a product of domestic social and economic institutions.

Baudin, Louis. FREE TRADE AND PEACE. Paris: International Institute of Intellectual Co-operation, 1939. 87 p.

Laissez-faire economics is not related directly either to peace or to war. War is a product of attitudes, not of economic systems.

Brodie, Bernard. WAR AND POLITICS. New York: Macmillan Co., 1973. 496 p.

In chapter 7 Brodie examines various theories on the causes of war and asserts that there is little foundation for the Marxist and neo-Marxist explanations of war.

Brown, Neville. "Underdevelopment as a Threat to World Peace." INTERNATIONAL AFFAIRS 47 (April 1971): 327-39.

Brown views the population explosion and rapid urbanization in the LDCs as potential threats to domestic and international peace.

Dougherty, James E., and Pfaltzgraff, Robert L., Jr. CONTENDING THEORIES OF INTERNATIONAL RELATIONS. New York: J.B. Lippincott Co., 1971. 416 p.

One of the best summaries of the theoretical literature on international relations. Chapter 6, "Economic Theories of Imperialism and War," presents a concise review of the Marxist theory of war and the major critics of that approach.

Ferris, Wayne. THE POWER CAPABILITIES OF NATION STATES: INTERNATIONAL CONFLICT AND WAR. Lexington, Mass.: Lexington Books, 1973. 185 p.

A sophisticated scientific investigation of the relationship between national power capabilities and international conflict.

Hawtrey, Ralph George. ECONOMIC ASPECTS OF SOVEREIGNTY. New York: Longmans, Green & Co., 1952. 191 p.

The cause of war is not found in economic imperialism but in the political structure of the international system--a structure in which security is found by each sovereign state maximizing its power. Power is related to the wealth of a state, and therefore states do attempt to maximize their economic interests. Economic development, however, is not an end in itself but a means to the ultimate end which is political survival.

Kara, Karel. "On the Marxist Theory of War and Peace." JOURNAL OF PEACE RESEARCH 5 (1968): 1-27.

A clear explanation of the Marxist view of interstate conflict and war.

Laski, Harold J. "The Economic Foundations of Peace." In THE INTELLIGENT

MAN'S WAY TO PREVENT WAR, edited by Leonard Woolf, pp. 499-548. London: Gollancz, 1933.

The main root of war lies in the economic imperialism pursued by capitalist states. The way to attack the problem of war is through social reforms that redistribute wealth within and between states.

Mallery, Otto T. ECONOMIC UNION AND DURABLE PEACE. New York: Harper Brothers, 1943. 183 p.

Argues that the most effective way of limiting or eliminating war is through the establishment of international economic union, a goal that can best be achieved by creating an international organization that facilitates free trade. "If goods cannot cross political frontiers, soldiers will."

Meade, James Edward. THE ECONOMIC BASIS FOR A DURABLE PEACE. London: George Allen & Unwin, 1940. 190 p.

Peace can only be maintained when there is a just and orderly international economic system. Meade offers several suggestions on how to establish an international economic organization that would help coordinate economic transactions of states. Some aspects of his proposals were later implemented with the establishment of the IMF.

Nef, John U. WAR AND HUMAN PROGRESS; AN ESSAY ON THE RISE OF INDUSTRIAL CIVILIZATION. Cambridge, Mass.: Harvard University Press, 1950. 464 p.

Traces the relationship between war and the technological development of society and finds that as the world has become more industrialized the problems of limiting war and its effects have become more difficult.

Pruitt, Dean G., and Snyder, Richard C., eds. THEORY AND RESEARCH ON THE CAUSES OF WAR. Englewood Cliffs, N.J.: Prentice-Hall, 1969. 314 p.

Includes numerous useful theoretical and empirical studies on the causes of war. The focus is primarily on political phenomena.

Robbins, Lionel. THE ECONOMIC CAUSES OF WAR. London: J. Cape; New York: Howard Fertig, 1968. 124 p.

Examines the Marxist explanation for war and finds that the historical facts do not support it. The cause of international conflict is the anarchic political system. International politics best explains war.

Seleznev, G.K. TRADE: A KEY TO PEACE AND PROGRESS. Translated from the Russian. Moscow: Progress Publishers, 1966. 134 p.

A Socialist account of contemporary international economic relations. The author argues that only Socialist economies can have
trade that is conducive to peace, for only such economies will
pursue trade on the basis of equality and mutual respect.

Staley, Eugene. WAR AND THE PRIVATE INVESTOR. New York: Howard
Fertig, 1967. 519 p.

First published in 1935, this landmark study remains one of the
most exhaustive investigations of the relationship of war to foreign
private investment. Staley's analysis leads him to the conclusion
that, while there is some association between war and economic
interests, politics is the real cause of international conflict.

Strachey, John. ON THE PREVENTION OF WAR. New York: St. Martin's
Press, 1963. 334 p.

Given the distribution of political power in the international system, the most effective way of preventing war is for the Soviet
Union and the United States to maintain a balance of power, ultimately shifting control of nuclear armaments to a combined au-
thority. If this shift is possible, further multilateralization of
power might occur. The only effective way of preventing war is
to modify the political structure of the contemporary international
system.

Viner, Jacob. "International Relations Between State-Controlled Economies."
In READINGS IN THE THEORY OF INTERNATIONAL TRADE, American Eco-
nomic Association, pp. 437-58. Blakiston Series of Republished Articles on
Economics, vol. 4. Philadelphia: Blakiston Co., 1949.

Argues that the extension of state control over national economies
will tend to increase international tensions and eventually lead to
the possibility of war. War is caused primarily by political tensions, and the best way to ensure peace is to avoid government
interference in the economy through a free enterprise system.

Youth and Student Division of the World Association of World Federalists.
WORLD PEACE THROUGH WORLD ECONOMY. New York: Humanities
Press, 1968. 147 p.

These papers, prepared for the Sixth International Study Conference
of the Youth Division of World Federalists, suggest that world
peace can be promoted through an improvement in economic conditions and increased economic cooperation.

Chapter 9

THE ECONOMICS OF WAR AND DEFENSE

An important dimension of national power is the economic potential of a state. Such a potential can be defined as a nation's productive capacity to meet both the private needs of people and the public necessities of the state, particularly national defense. The ability of a state to satisfy both of these needs is of course related to the nation's overall level of economic development and more particularly to such conditions as industrial capacity, access to raw materials, technological development, infrastructure, and communication and transportation networks. The first two parts of this chapter are concerned with defense economics and wartime economic mobilization, the domestic economics of defense. The first theme focuses on the peacetime relationship of economic productivity and national defense costs and procurement; the second theme is concerned with the economics of mobilization in time of war. It is desirable to separate wartime and peacetime defense economics because of the unusual economic problems created in time of war, when productive resources are transformed to meet the military needs of the state. The third part of this chapter focuses on warfare economics, the international economics of war and defense. Since economic power is an integral component of military power, one of the means of waging war is by curbing the economic capacity of a foreign state either by creating domestic economic dislocations or by limiting necessary imports.

A. DEFENSE ECONOMICS

Baldwin, John. "The Economics of Peace and War: A Simulation." JOURNAL OF CONFLICT RESOLUTION 11 (December 1967): 383-97.

> Baldwin develops a game highlighting the strategies of theft and exchange (war and trade) used by actors to obtain goods from others. The game is then used to develop economic implications for defense strategies.

Baldwin, William L. THE STRUCTURE OF THE DEFENSE MARKET, 1955-1964. Durham, N.C.: Duke University Press, 1967. 249 p.

Benoit, Emile. DEFENSE AND ECONOMIC GROWTH IN DEVELOPING COUNTRIES. Lexington, Mass.: Lexington Books, 1973. 310 p.

This statistical study of defense expenditures and economic growth found that the two variables were related during the 1950-65 period but that it was impossible to determine the nature of the relationship or the extent of causality.

_____. "The Economic Impact of Disarmament in the United States." In DISARMAMENT: ITS POLITICS AND ECONOMICS, edited by Seymour Melman, pp. 134-57. Boston: American Academy of Arts and Sciences, 1962.

Summarizes the findings of a year's research on the economic impact of disarmament in the United States.

_____. "The Economics of Disarmament and Coexistence." In ECONOMICS AND THE IDEAS OF MANKIND, edited by Bert F. Hoselitz, pp. 237-77. New York: Columbia University Press, 1965.

_____, ed. DISARMAMENT AND WORLD ECONOMIC INTERDEPENDENCE. New York: Columbia University Press, 1967. 260 p.

A collection of papers given at the 1965 Conference on Economic Aspects of World Disarmament and Interdependence in Oslo, Norway. The articles examine different dimensions of national defense, arms control, and disarmament.

Benoit, Emile, and Lubell, Harold. "World Defense Expenditures." JOURNAL OF PEACE RESEARCH 3 (1966): 97-113.

An excellent source of comparative defense expenditure data.

Benoit, Emile, and Boulding, Kenneth E., eds. DISARMAMENT AND THE ECONOMY. New York: Harper & Row, 1963. 306 p.

The underlying theme of these essays is that disarmament, while posing numerous economic problems, will not bring about a complete economic depression. Many of the domestic and international adjustments required for defense cutbacks are discussed.

Bernard, Stephen. "Some Political and Technical Implications of Disarmament." WORLD POLITICS 8 (October 1965): 71-90.

Examines the feasibility of disarmament during the cold war era of the 1950s and concludes that disarmament itself would not guarantee peace.

Bidwell, Percy W. ECONOMIC DEFENSE OF LATIN AMERICA. Boston: World Peace Foundation, 1941. 96 p.

A study of U.S.-Latin American economic relations during the early 1940s. Bidwell suggests that, given the threat of Nazi conquest of Latin America, the most effective way of helping the South-

ern Hemisphere is by assisting Great Britain in defeating Hitler.
Economic interests with Latin America are of secondary importance.

_____. RAW MATERIALS; A STUDY OF AMERICAN POLICY. Published for
the Council on Foreign Relations. New York: Harper & Row, 1958. xvi,
403 p.

An exhaustive study of the postwar raw materials policy of the
United States, with case studies of lead, zinc, copper, nickel,
iron and steel, wool, rubber, and oil. Policy recommendations
are offered in the last chapter.

Bidwell, Percy W., and Upgren, Arthur R. "A Trade Policy for National
Defense." FOREIGN AFFAIRS 19 (January 1941): 282-96.

Bolton, Roger E., ed. DEFENSE AND DISARMAMENT: THE ECONOMICS
OF TRANSITION. Englewood Cliffs, N.J.: Prentice-Hall, 1966. viii,
180 p.

Bolton suggests that the economic impact of disarmament is likely
to encourage economic growth. Until significant defense reductions are implemented, the United States should encourage efficiency in its defense operations and prepare the way for major
reductions at a later date.

Boulding, Kenneth E., ed. PEACE AND THE WAR INDUSTRY. Chicago:
Aldine Publishing Co., 1970. 159 p.

Two essays in this anthology on peace and military expenditures
are of particular interest: K. Boulding's introduction and Raoul
Naroll's study "Does Military Deterrence Deter?"

Center for Strategic Studies. Georgetown University. ECONOMIC IMPACT
OF THE VIETNAM WAR. Special Report Series, no. 5. New York: Renais-
sance Editions, 1967. xii, 86 p.

Prepared by a group of distinguished economists, this study examines the general relationship between military expenditures and
economic growth. Some specific effects of the Vietnam war on
the U.S. economy are discussed.

Cobb, Stephen. "Defense Spending and Foreign Policy in the House of Repre-
sentatives." JOURNAL OF CONFLICT RESOLUTION 13 (September 1969):
358-69.

Cobb examines and subsequently rejects the validity of the thesis
that congressmen from districts economically dependent on defense
spending are more likely to support aggressive belligerent foreign
policies than congressmen from other districts.

Condliffe, J.B. "Economic Power as an Instrument of National Policy." AMERICAN ECONOMIC ASSOCIATION PAPERS AND PROCEEDINGS 34 (March 1944): 305-14.

An impressionistic comparative analysis of the economic power of the United States relative to other world powers as of 1944.

_____. WAR AND DEPRESSION. Boston and New York: World Peace Foundation, 1935. 35 p.

Argues that war brings about detrimental economic effects because it limits trade and credit and disorganizes the patterns of production.

Dunn, John. "American Dependence on Materials Imports: The Worldwide Resource Base." JOURNAL OF CONFLICT RESOLUTION 4 (March 1960): 106-22.

Examines various policies for assuring the availability of strategic raw materials in wartime and concludes that there is no single policy that can do this. An effective policy must be comprehensive, dealing with domestic and international production and consumption patterns.

Dyckman, John W. "Some Regional Development Issues in Defense Program Shifts." JOURNAL OF PEACE RESEARCH 1 (1964): 191-203.

Since defense expenditures affect the economic development of some regions more than of others, defense cutbacks will similarly make some regions more vulnerable than others. In order to deal with this problem, Dyckman examines the feasibility of creating a program to offset the negative consequences of defense cutbacks.

Falk, Richard A., and Mendlovitz, Saul H., eds. DISARMAMENT AND ECONOMIC DEVELOPMENT. The Strategy of World Order, vol. 4. New York: World Law Fund, 1966. 672 p.

A collection of theoretical essays on the political economy of disarmament.

Feinstein, Otto. "Disarmament: Economic Effect." CURRENT HISTORY 47 (August 1964): 81-87.

A general discussion of some of the economic problems posed by defense cutbacks.

Fieser, Max E. ECONOMIC POLICY AND WAR POTENTIAL. Washington, D.C.: Public Affairs Press, 1964. 136 p.

Fishman, Leo, and Fishman, Betty G. "Disarmament: How Will the Economy Respond?" QUARTERLY REVIEW OF ECONOMIC BUSINESS 2 (August 1962): 15-24.

The economic effects of disarmament can be significant if arms reductions are begun during periods of slow economic growth and high
unemployment. Defense cutbacks should be started ideally only
under conditions of economic health.

Friedman, Milton. "Price, Income, and Monetary Changes in Three Wartime
Periods." AMERICAN ECONOMIC REVIEW: PAPERS AND PROCEEDINGS 42
(May 1952): 612-25.

Gottheil, Fred M. "An Economic Assessment of the Military Burden in the
Middle East, 1960-1980." JOURNAL OF CONFLICT RESOLUTION 18 (September 1974): 502-13.

Attempts to measure the economic burden of military expenditures
in Israel, Jordan, Egypt, Syria, and Iraq using sophisticated tools
of mathematical analysis.

Hardt, John P.; Stolzenbach, C. Darwin; and Kohn, Martin J. THE COLD
WAR ECONOMIC GAP; THE INCREASING THREAT TO AMERICAN SUPREM-
ACY. New York: Praeger Publishers, 1961. 114 p.

A summary of the major findings of 1959 Congressional hearings on
the comparative power of the U.S. and the Soviet economies.

Harris, Seymour E. THE ECONOMICS OF AMERICAN DEFENSE. New York:
W.W. Norton, 1941. 350 p.

Examines domestic and international economic problems and policies
relating to American security during the 1930s. Useful primarily
for historical purposes.

Hart, Albert G. DEFENSE WITHOUT INFLATION, WITH RECOMMENDATIONS
OF THE COMMITTEE ON ECONOMIC STABILIZATION. New York: Twentieth Century Fund, 1951. ix, 186 p.

Written during the early part of the cold war, this study encourages the development of a strong U.S. economy by increasing
productivity and decreasing inflation. Various proposals are offered on how to limit inflation while also maintaining high levels
of defense spending. Most recommendations are out of date.

_____. "General Strategy of Economic Policy for Less-than-Total War."
AMERICAN ECONOMIC REVIEW 41 (March 1951): 55-59.

Hart, Albert G., and Brown, E. Cary; with H.F. Kasmussen. FINANCING
DEFENSE; FEDERAL TAX AND EXPENDITURE POLICIES, WITH POLICY REC-
OMMENDATIONS BY THE COMMITTEE ON ECONOMIC STABILIZATION.
New York: Twentieth Century Fund, 1951. 161 p.

Recommendations are offered on how federal revenues can be increased in peacetime to meet the necessary costs of mobilization without inflation.

Hirschman, Albert O. NATIONAL POWER AND THE STRUCTURE OF FOR-EIGN TRADE. Berkeley and Los Angeles: University of California Press, 1945. 170 p.

This pioneering study remains the most rigorous analysis of the relationship between trade and national power. Using theory (part 1) and historical and empirical evidence (part 2) as his base, Hirschman argues that the only method of diminishing the effectiveness of trade as an instrument of national power is to restrict the power of states. To do this, national economic sovereignty must be curbed through "internalization of power."

Hitch, Charles J., and McKean, Ronald N. THE ECONOMICS OF DEFENSE IN THE NUCLEAR AGE. Cambridge, Mass.: Harvard University Press, 1960. 422 p.

The writers, both economists formerly at the RAND Corporation, discuss how the tools of economic analysis can be applied to matters of national defense. Special problems of defense economics, such as economic warfare, mobilization, research and development, and the economics of military alliances, are also examined.

Hutchins, John G.B. "The Effect of the Civil War and Two World Wars on American Transportation." AMERICAN ECONOMIC REVIEW: PAPERS AND PROCEEDINGS 42 (May 1952): 626-38.

Knorr, Klaus. "The Concept of Economic Potential for War." WORLD POLITICS 10 (October 1957): 49-62.

Tries to revive the concept of economic war potential by emphasizing its predictive and manipulative value. Despite the development of nuclear weapons, economic capability is still an important component of national defense.

_____. MILITARY POWER AND POTENTIAL. Lexington, Mass.: D.C. Heath & Co., 1970. 150 p.

A theoretical study of the nature and use of military power in the international system. Chapter 3 provides an insightful discussion of the economic basis of national power.

_____. POWER AND WEALTH: THE POLITICAL ECONOMY OF INTERNATIONAL POWER. New York: Basic Books, 1973. 198 p.

Examines how power and influence can be obtained and used in the international system, focusing specifically on military and economic power and the relationship between the two.

Lauterbach, Albert T. ECONOMICS IN UNIFORM: MILITARY ECONOMY AND SOCIAL STRUCTURE. Princeton, N.J.: Princeton University Press, 1943. 278 p.

A comparative analysis of the German and Anglo-American social structures and economic policies before and during the Second World War. Of particular interest is chapter 8 on economic warfare policies of the United States, England, and Japan. An excellent bibliography is included.

Leontief, Wassily. "Disarmament, Foreign Aid, and Economic Growth." JOURNAL OF PEACE RESEARCH 1 (1964): 155–67.

A highly sophisticated examination of the possible economic effects of disarmament and foreign aid.

Leontief, Wassily, and Hoffenberg, M. "The Economic Effects of Disarmament." SCIENTIFIC AMERICAN 24 (April 1961): 47–55.

Leontief, Wassily, et al. "The Economic Impact--Industrial and Regional--of an Arms Cut." REVIEW OF ECONOMICS AND STATISTICS 47 (August 1965): 217–41.

Using input-output analysis, this study examines the effect of defense cutbacks accompanied by increased nondefense expenditures on the industrial composition and regional distribution of employment.

Lincoln, George A. ECONOMICS OF NATIONAL SECURITY: MANAGING AMERICA'S RESOURCES FOR DEFENSE. 2d ed. New York: Prentice-Hall, 1954. 620 p.

One of the best postwar texts on the subject of the American economy and national defense. Parts 3 and 4 examines wartime domestic and international economic policies for defensive and offensive purposes.

McKean, Roland N., ed. ISSUES IN DEFENSE ECONOMICS. New York: National Bureau of Economic Research, 1967. 286 p.

This collection of theoretical articles, originally prepared for a conference on the economic dimension of defense, deals with three issues: the applicability of economic concepts to defense problems, strategies of defense, and institutional structures and defense spending.

Mason, Edward S. "American Security and Access to Raw Materials." WORLD POLITICS 1 (January 1949): 147–60.

Examines how the access and availability of raw materials affects national security in general and military power in particular.

Melman, Seymour. THE PERMANENT WAR ECONOMY: AMERICAN CAPI-
TALISM IN DECLINE. New York: Simon & Schuster, 1974. 371 p.

Discounting the traditional Marxist interpretations, Melman asserts
that the war economy of the United States is not a consequence
of its capitalistic system, but rather the result of its politico-social
structure. Suggestions for shifting the economy away from militarism are offered.

_____, ed. THE DEFENSE ECONOMY; CONVERSION OF INDUSTRIES AND
OCCUPATIONS TO CIVILIAN NEEDS. New York: Praeger Publishers, 1970.
518 p.

These essays examine how different sectors of the U.S. economy
would be affected by a significant drop in military spending. An
excellent annotated bibliography is included.

_____. DISARMAMENT: ITS POLITICS AND ECONOMICS. Boston: Amer-
ican Academy of Arts and Sciences, 1962. 398 p.

The articles, prepared originally for a research conference on disarmament at Columbia University, examine issues relating to the
theory and practice of disarmament. Two essays particularly are
of interest: "The Economic Impact of Disarmament in the U.S."
by Emile Benoit, and "Problems of Industrial Conversion" by
Richard C. Raymond.

_____. THE WAR ECONOMY OF THE UNITED STATES; READINGS ON
MILITARY INDUSTRY AND ECONOMY. New York: St. Martin's Press, 1971.
xiii, 247 p.

A collection of some of the most important contemporary studies
on U.S. defense economics. The essays deal with four themes:
the scale of military economy, the industrial firm, economic consequences of military expenditures, and peacetime industry conversion.

Members of Congress for Peace Through Law, Military Spending Committee.
THE ECONOMICS OF DEFENSE; A BIPARTISAN REVIEW OF MILITARY SPEND-
ING. New York: Praeger Publishers, 1971. 256 p.

An analysis of the major U.S. hardware and manpower defense
needs and expenditures for the 1971 fiscal year. The research
was undertaken "in the conviction that reductions can be made
in military spending without any corresponding weakening of national security."

Nadler, Eugene B. "Some Economic Disadvantages of the Arms Race." JOUR-
NAL OF CONFLICT RESOLUTION 7 (September 1963): 503-8.

Outlines some of the principal social, political, and economic
costs of U.S. defense expenditures.

O'Neal, Russell D. "Industry, Society, and Arms Control." JOURNAL OF CONFLICT RESOLUTION 7 (September 1963): 464-68.

> The author, a business executive, discusses how the business community can assist the arms control process in the United States.

Ono, Giichi. EXPENDITURES OF THE SINO-JAPANESE WAR. New York: Oxford University Press, 1922. 330 p.

> An exhaustive examination of the economic effects of the Sino-Japanese War.

_____. WAR AND ARMAMENT EXPENDITURES OF JAPAN. New York: Oxford University Press, 1922. 314 p.

> A historical analysis of Japan's defense expenditures during the latter part of the nineteenth century with some assessment as to their impact on the national economy.

Rosen, Steven [J.], ed. TESTING THE THEORY OF THE MILITARY INDUSTRIAL COMPLEX. Lexington, Mass.: Lexington Books, 1973. x, 311 p.

> A useful collection of theoretical and empirical studies on the political economy of military defense. All essays except one (chapter 5, "The Soviet Military Industrial Complex: Does it Exist?") deal with the U.S. defense program.

Schilling, Warner R. "The Politics of National Defense: Fiscal 1950." In STRATEGY, POLITICS, AND DEFENSE BUDGETS, edited by Warner R. Schilling, Paul Y. Hammond, and Glen H. Snyder, pp. 5-266. New York: Columbia University Press, 1962.

> Examines the political dynamics of the preparation, development, and approval of the 1950 U.S. defense budget. An excellent case study on the domestic politics of military defense policy.

Schlesinger, James R. THE POLITICAL ECONOMY OF NATIONAL SECURITY; A STUDY OF THE ECONOMIC ASPECTS OF THE CONTEMPORARY POWER STRUGGLE. New York: Praeger Publishers, 1960. 287 p.

> A general theoretical analysis of the political economy of cold war national security in the United States. Schlesinger argues for hard-line military and economic policies vis-a-vis the Soviet Union.

Snyder, Glen H. STOCKPILING STRATEGIC MATERIALS; POLITICS AND NATIONAL DEFENSE. San Francisco: Chandler Publishing Co., 1966. xii, 314 p.

> A historical account of the U.S. postwar strategic materials program focusing on the political forces that have influenced the

development of the program. The objective is to develop a body of empirical knowledge on the politics of national defense.

Udis, Bernard, ed. THE ECONOMIC CONSEQUENCES OF REDUCED MILITARY SPENDING. Lexington, Mass.: Lexington Books, 1973. ix, 398 p.

These papers, prepared originally for the U.S. Arms Control and Disarmament Agency, analyze different aspects of defense cutbacks.

U.S. Arms Control and Disarmament Agency. ECONOMIC IMPACT OF REDUCTIONS IN DEFENSE SPENDING. Washington, D.C.: Government Printing Office, 1972. 28 p.

A brief study summarizing some twenty-nine research projects on the impact of defense expenditure reductions. The study deals with four themes: the national economy, selected industries, regions and communities, and the individual worker.

_____. WORLD MILITARY EXPENDITURES, 1969, AND RELATED DATA FOR 120 COUNTRIES. Washington, D.C.: Government Printing Office, 1969. 26 p.

Vernon, Raymond. "Foreign Trade and National Defense." FOREIGN AFFAIRS 34 (October 1955): 77-88.

Suggests that the U.S. cold war national security program encourages autarky, a policy that is counterproductive to the real interests of U.S. security. In a nuclear age the best economic preparation for war is a strong program of economic cooperation with allies, not a policy of self-sufficiency.

Wallace, Donald H. ECONOMIC CONTROLS AND DEFENSE. New York: Twentieth Century Fund, 1953. 260 p.

A study of how to protect the American system from two economic pressures--inflation and direct controls--which result from a high level of defense expenditures.

Weidenbaum, Murray L. "Could the U.S. Afford Disarmament?" In THE CHANGING AMERICAN ECONOMY, edited by John R. Coleman, pp. 170-81. New York: Basic Books, 1967.

Suggests that the United States could significantly reduce its military expenditures without major detrimental effects to the national economy. The principal policy decision needed in the event of disarmament is to determine whether the whole economy or selected regions of high defense expenditures will bear the costs of the shift.

_____. "The Defense Business: A Far Cry from Adam Smith." CHALLENGE 14 (May-June 1966): 35-44.

Examines the relationship of government to private business in
defense-oriented firms, and suggests that new approaches to defense production might yield higher net gains for the nation.

_____. THE ECONOMICS OF PEACETIME DEFENSE. New York: Praeger
Publishers, 1974. 193 p.

A careful analysis of the role of the military-industrial complex
within the U.S. economy by one of the foremost authorities on
U.S. defense economics.

B. WARTIME ECONOMIC MOBILIZATION

Bloch, Henry S., and Hoselitz, Bert F. ECONOMICS OF MILITARY OCCU-
PATION: SELECTED PROBLEMS. Chicago: Foundation Press, 1944. 130 p.

A discussion of economic issues and problems peculiar to a nation
under military occupation·

Bowley, Arthur L. SOME ECONOMIC CONSEQUENCES OF THE GREAT
WAR. London: Thornton and Butterworth, 1930. 252 p.

Examines the major economic effects of the First World War on
the United Kingdom and to a lesser extent on France and Germany.

Campbell, W. Glenn. ECONOMICS OF MOBILIZATION AND WAR. Homewood, Ill.: Richard D. Irwin, 1952. iv, 196 p.

Chandler, Lester V., and Wallace, Donald H., eds. ECONOMIC MOBILIZA-
TION AND STABILIZATION; SELECTED MATERIALS ON THE ECONOMICS
OF WAR AND DEFENSE. New York: Henry Holt and Co., 1951. 605 p.

A useful anthology on wartime economic problems and policies,
drawing heavily on the experience of the United States during
the Second World War.

Clark, John J. THE NEW ECONOMICS OF NATIONAL DEFENSE. New
York: Random House, 1966. 235 p.

The best up-to-date study on economics and national defense.
The most useful chapters focus on the application of game theory
(chapter 3) and the theory of conflict (chapter 4) to international
relations, and on the methods and approaches of economic warfare
(chapter 5). The analysis of the relationship of economic growth
and war (chapter 6) is illuminating. Helpful bibliographical annotations follow each chapter.

Clark, John M.; Hamilton, Walton H.; and Moulton, Harold G. READINGS
IN THE ECONOMICS OF WAR. Chicago: University of Chicago Press, 1918.
676 p.

A comprehensive early twentieth-century anthology on the economics of war.

Clayton, James L., ed. THE ECONOMIC IMPACT OF THE COLD WAR; SOURCES AND READINGS. New York: Harcourt, Brace and World, 1970. 287 p.

These essays examine different effects of the cold war on the U.S. economy, including the impact on research and development and on institutional structures. One group of articles deals with the impact of the Vietnam war on the American system.

Gold, Bela. WARTIME ECONOMIC PLANNING IN AGRICULTURE; A STUDY IN THE ALLOCATION OF RESOURCES. New York: Columbia University Press, 1949. 594 p.

A painstaking analysis of the agricultural mobilization program of the United States during the Second World War, focusing on specific commodities and sectors of the agrarian economy.

Harris, Seymour E. THE ECONOMICS OF MOBILIZATION AND INFLATION. 1951. Reprint. New York: Greenwood Press, 1968. 308 p.

Hirst, Francis W. THE CONSEQUENCES OF WAR TO GREAT BRITAIN. New Haven, Conn.: Yale University Press, 1934. 311 p.

A historical account of the major political, social, and economic consequences of the First World War on Great Britain.

Holden, Greenville. "Rationing and Exchange Control in British War Finance." QUARTERLY JOURNAL OF ECONOMICS 54 (Fall 1940): 171-200.

Homan, P.T. "Economics in the War Period." AMERICAN ECONOMIC REVIEW 36 (December 1946): 855-71.

Janeway, Eliot. THE STRUGGLE FOR SURVIVAL; A CHRONICLE OF ECONOMIC MOBILIZATION IN WORLD WAR II. New Haven, Conn.: Yale University Press, 1951. 382 p.

A descriptive account of U.S. economic policies during the Second World War.

McGuire, S.H. "Economic Mobilization, A New Field of Study." ANNALS OF THE AMERICAN ACADEMY OF POLITICAL AND SOCIAL SCIENCE 278 (November 1951): 83-87.

A brief outline of the important issues of wartime economic mobilization and the problem of conversion to a peacetime economy.

Mendershausen, Horst. THE ECONOMICS OF WAR. Rev. ed. New York: Prentice-Hall, 1943. 380 p.

> One of the popular texts on warfare economics written during the early part of the Second World War. Particularly useful is the analysis of the international economics of war as it relates to allied, neutral, and belligerent nations.

Neal, Alfred D., ed. INTRODUCTION TO WAR ECONOMICS. Chicago: Richard D. Irwin, 1942. 248 p.

> Although much of the material in this text is out of date, the study provides a useful guide to the major issues and problems of wartime economics.

Pigou, A.C. THE POLITICAL ECONOMY OF WAR. Rev. ed. New York: Macmillan Co., 1941. 168 p.

> Originally published in 1921, this treatise is one of the outstanding analytical studies on the war economy. The first two chapters examine the relationship of military preparedness to the national economy and the economic causes of war. The major portion of the study deals with specific economic problems of war.

Rosenbaum, E.M. "War Economics: A Bibliographical Approach." ECONOMICA 9 (February 1942): 64-95.

> A bibliographical analysis of war economics based on materials published prior to 1942. An excellent source for early twentieth-century materials on the subject.

Silberner, Edmond. THE PROBLEMS OF WAR IN NINETEENTH CENTURY ECONOMIC THOUGHT. Translated by Alexander H. Krappe. Princeton, N.J.: Princeton University Press, 1946. 332 p.

> An excellent study of the theories of selected nineteenth-century thinkers on warfare economics.

Spiegel, Henry W. THE ECONOMICS OF TOTAL WAR. New York: Appleton-Century Co., 1942. 389 p.

> A general text on war economics. Chapter 11 examines the international economics of wartime.

Stein, Emanuel, and Backman, Jules, eds. WAR ECONOMICS. New York: Farrar and Rinehart, 1942. 494 p.

> A general anthology on the economics of war.

Tobin, Harold J., and Bidwell, Percy W. MOBILIZING CIVILIAN AMERICA. New York: Council on Foreign Relations, 1940. 268 p.

A study of the American military and economic mobilization during the First World War and of the wartime planning during the interwar period. Chapters 7 and 8 examine the wartime mobilization of labor and business.

Woodlief, Thomas. "Lessons of War Finance." AMERICAN ECONOMIC REVIEW 41 (September 1951): 618-31.

Wright, Chester W., ed. ECONOMIC PROBLEMS OF WAR AND ITS AFTERMATH. Chicago: University of Chicago Press, 1942. 190 p.

A collection of seven lectures, originally given under the auspices of the Charles R. Walgreen Foundation, on various aspects of the war economy.

C. ECONOMIC WARFARE

Abbott, C.C. "Economic Defense of the United States." HARVARD BUSINESS REVIEW 26 (September 1948): 613-26.

Reviews economic strategies foreign states could use against the United States to bring about inflation, instability, and other economic problems. Abbott discusses defensive measures to counter such policies.

_____. "Economic Penetration and Power Politics." HARVARD BUSINESS REVIEW 26 (July 1948): 410-24.

An analysis of the economic instruments available for manipulating the business and economic affairs of another state.

Adler-Karlsson, Gunner. WESTERN ECONOMIC WARFARE, 1947-1967; A CASE STUDY IN FOREIGN POLICY. Stockholm: Humanities Press, 1968. xv, 319 p.

An excellent study of the postwar economic warfare policies and practices of the United States and Western European states against the Communist nations. The major emphasis is on embargo policies. Where possible, an attempt is made to quantify the effects of economic pressures on domestic economies.

Allen, Robert L. SOVIET ECONOMIC WARFARE. Washington, D.C.: Public Affairs Press, 1965. 293 p.

Allen examines the Soviet Union's postwar economic policies in an attempt to show that they are simply tools to promote the state's political objectives. See particularly chapter 5, "Political Motives and Goals."

Baldwin, H.W. "Hitler Can Be Defeated; Economic Measures." NEW YORK TIMES, 15 June 1941, p. 3.

Basch, Antonin. THE NEW ECONOMIC WARFARE. New York: Columbia University Press, 1941. 190 p.

> A study of the economic dimensions of the early part of the Second World War, focusing on the economic preparation for war, the adaptation of national economies to total war, and the practice of economic warfare.

Bidwell, Percy W. "Our Economic Warfare." FOREIGN AFFAIRS 20 (April 1942): 421-37.

> An overview of some of the major aspects of U.S. economic warfare policies during the Second World War.

Culbertson, W.S. "Total Economic Warfare." ANNALS OF THE AMERICAN ACADEMY OF POLITICAL AND SOCIAL SCIENCE 222 (July 1942): 8-12.

> A brief analysis of the relationship of economic strength and military potential.

Einzig, Paul. ECONOMIC WARFARE. London: Macmillan & Co., 1940. 151 p.

> Examines the means and methods of defensive and offensive economic warfare and then assesses the potential economic strength of some of the major world powers on the eve of the Second World War. Einzig asserts that Western democracies are economically more powerful than totalitarian systems.

Freedman, Robert Owen. ECONOMIC WARFARE IN THE COMMUNIST BLOC; A STUDY OF SOVIET ECONOMIC PRESSURE AGAINST YUGOSLAVIA, ALBANIA, AND COMMUNIST CHINA. New York: Praeger Publishers, 1970. 192 p.

> Using as a base his analysis of the Soviet Union's economic warfare practices against Albania, Yugoslavia, and Communist China, Freedman concludes that economic pressures have great limitations and are often counterproductive. "All in all, although economic pressure may appear to be a potent weapon in the hands of an economically powerful nation, in reality its usefulness as an instrument of policy is very limited indeed."

Gordon, David L., and Dangerfield, Roy. THE HIDDEN WEAPON; THE STORY OF ECONOMIC WARFARE. New York: Harper & Row, 1947. xii, 238 p.

> A general account of the Anglo-American economic warfare practices toward the Axis powers during the Second World War.

Hillman, H.C. "Analysis of Germany's Foreign Trade and the War." ECO-NOMICA 7 (February 1940): 66-88.

> Examines the domestic and foreign structure of Germany's economy with a view of assessing the probable impact of the Allied economic blockade.

Jack, D.T. STUDIES IN ECONOMIC WARFARE. London: P.S. King and Son, 1940. 178 p.

> A historical account of the methods and techniques of economic warfare from the early nineteenth century through the beginning of the Second World War. Chapter 2 examines the development of international law pertinent to such warfare.

Olson, Richard S. "Economic Coercion in International Disputes: The United States and Peru in the I.P.C. Expropriation Disputes of 1968-1971." JOURNAL OF DEVELOPING AREAS 9 (April 1975): 395-414.

> A study of the indirect economic sanctions applied by the United States on Peru following the expropriation of the International Petroleum Company. Olson suggests that the economic dependency of LDCs on the industrial, developed states makes them vulnerable to indirect economic sanctions.

Polk, Judd. "Freezing Dollars Against the Axis." FOREIGN AFFAIRS 20 (October 1941): 113-30.

Schreiber, Anna P. "Economic Coercion as an Instrument of Foreign Policy: U.S. Economic Measures Against Cuba and the Dominican Republic." WORLD POLITICS 25 (April 1973): 387-413.

> Schreiber argues that economic coercion against Cuba and the Dominican Republic was helpful in achieving some U.S. foreign policy objectives, although there were some unintended results as well. The major function of economic coercion is symbolic, and its ultimate effectiveness will depend on support from political and military policies.

Thorp, Willard L. "American Policy and the Soviet Economic Offensive." FOREIGN AFFAIRS 35 (January 1957): 271-82.

> Analyzes important shifts in the Soviet Union's postwar economic policies in order to define policy implications for the United States.

Tucker, Robert W. "Oil: The Issue of American Intervention." COMMENTARY 59 (January 1975): 21-31.

> Evaluates possible policies the United States could pursue toward

the effective cartel established by the oil-producing countries.
Military power is not a viable policy alternative.

Wu, Yuan-Li. ECONOMIC WARFARE. New York: Prentice-Hall, 1952.
388 p.

A comprehensive introduction to the subject of economic warfare.

Chapter 10

OTHER REFERENCE MATERIALS

In this chapter two types of information sources are included: bibliographies and journals. The bibliographies themselves vary in terms of scope and purpose; some of them deal with a limited theme of international relations while others focus on the entire discipline of either economics or political science. Some bibliographies are concerned with reference materials only. Journals of particular importance have been asterisked.

A. BIBLIOGRAPHIES

ABC POL SCI; ADVANCE BIBLIOGRAPHY OF CONTENTS: POLITICAL SCIENCE AND GOVERNMENT. Santa Barbara, Calif.: Clio Press, 1969--. Nine issues per year.

> A bibliography of current issues of leading domestic and foreign journals in law, politics, and other social sciences. The purpose of the bibliographical journal is to provide in advance a listing of the articles being published. No annotations.

Brock, Clifton. THE LITERATURE OF POLITICAL SCIENCE; A GUIDE FOR STUDENTS, LIBRARIANS AND TEACHERS. New York: R.R. Bowker Co., 1969. xii, 232 p.

> Probably the most complete introductory guide to information sources in political science. Part 1 examines the principal types of information sources for studying politics; part 2 lists the principal bibliographies and other reference sources useful in research in the many subfields of the discipline.

Burtis, David, et al., eds. MULTINATIONAL CORPORATION-NATION-STATE INTERACTION: AN ANNOTATED BIBLIOGRAPHY. Philadelphia: Foreign Policy Research Institute, 1971. 290 p.

> An excellent annotated bibliography of 714 books and articles on the political economy of the MNC.

Deutsch, Karl W., and Merritt, Richard. NATIONALISM AND NATIONAL DEVELOPMENT: AN INTERDISCIPLINARY BIBLIOGRAPHY. Cambridge, Mass.: M.I.T. Press, 1970. 519 p.

> A comprehensive listing of books, pamphlets, and articles on nationalism and development. Sections 8 and 10 cover literature on imperialism and political integration.

Dexter, Byron, ed. THE FOREIGN AFFAIRS 50-YEAR BIBLIOGRAPHY; NEW EVALUATIONS OF SIGNIFICANT BOOKS ON INTERNATIONAL RELATIONS, 1920-1970. Published for the Council on Foreign Relations. New York: R.R. Bowker Co., 1972. xxvii, 936 p.

> Noted social scientists evaluate 2,130 of the most significant books published on international relations during the 1920-70 period. A helpful aid, although the number of books on international economic relations is not extensive.

ECONOMICS SELECTIONS: AN INTERNATIONAL BIBLIOGRAPHY. SERIES I: NEW BOOKS IN ECONOMICS. New York: Gordon and Breach Science Publishers, 1953--. Quarterly.

> An annotated bibliography of new books, pamphlets, and articles in the various subfields of economics, including international economic relations. An excellent bibliographical source.

ECONOMICS SELECTIONS: AN INTERNATIONAL BIBLIOGRAPHY. SERIES II: BASIC LISTS IN SPECIAL FIELDS. New York: Gordon and Breach Science Publishers. Irregular.

> Designed to assist in building collections in particular subfields of economics. See in particular the 1968 "Special Bibliography in International Economics."

FOREIGN AFFAIRS BIBLIOGRAPHY; A SELECTED AND ANNOTATED LIST OF BOOKS ON INTERNATIONAL RELATIONS, 1952-1962. Published for the Council on Foreign Relations. New York: R.R. Bowker Co., 1964.

> Good organization and annotations make this volume an excellent bibliographical aid. Besides the current volume, there are previous studies covering the 1919-32, 1932-42, and 1942-52 periods.

Gould, Wesley L., and Barkun, Michael. SOCIAL SCIENCE LITERATURE; A BIBLIOGRAPHY FOR INTERNATIONAL LAW. Published for the American Society of International Law. Princeton, N.J.: Princeton University Press, 1972. xiii, 641 p.

> A comprehensive annotated bibliography of social science literature relevant to the study of international law. Chapter 8 deals with international economic issues, including foreign investment and economic assistance as they pertain to international law.

Harmon, Robert B. POLITICAL SCIENCE; A BIBLIOGRAPHICAL GUIDE TO THE LITERATURE. New York: Scarecrow Press, 1965. 388 p.

A general bibliographical guide to the field of politics, a sub-stantial portion of which is devoted to international relations and foreign policy. Two supplements have been published, one in 1968 and the other in 1972.

Holler, Frederick. THE INFORMATION SOURCES OF POLITICAL SCIENCE. Santa Barbara, Calif.: ABC-CLIO, 1971. viii, 264 p.

A useful guide to the important bibliographies, dictionaries, and other reference works used in political research. Chapter 7 deals with information sources in international relations.

INTERNATIONAL BIBLIOGRAPHY OF ECONOMICS. Chicago: Aldine Pub-lishing Co., 1952--. Annual.

An exhaustive classified bibliography on economics covering books, articles, and other documents from all nations. The volumes are prepared by the International Committee for Social Science Docu-mentation under the direction of UNESCO. No annotations.

INTERNATIONAL BIBLIOGRAPHY OF POLITICAL SCIENCE. Chicago: Aldine Publishing Co., 1953--. Annual.

A comprehensive classified bibliography of international political science materials. Each volume covers some 4,000 entries; there is generally a lag of at least two years between original publica-tion and citation here. No annotations.

Larson, Arthur D. NATIONAL SECURITY AFFAIRS: A GUIDE TO INFORMA-TION SOURCES. Detroit: Gale Research Co., 1973. 411 p.

A useful compilation of bibliographical sources on American na-tional security. Some attention is given to the economic dimen-sions of defense.

Mason, John B. INTERNATIONAL RELATIONS & RECENT HISTORY; IN-DEXES, ABSTRACTS & PERIODICALS. Research Resources; Annotated Guide to the Social Sciences, vol. 1. Santa Barbara, Calif.: ABC-CLIO, 1968. 243 p.

The most complete annotated bibliographical guide on the major sources of information in international relations. The guide cov-ers indexes and abstracts, periodicals, bibliographies, government publications, and newspapers. A helpful guide to the study of international political economy.

Pogany, Andras H., and Pogany, Hortenzia Lers. POLITICAL SCIENCE AND INTERNATIONAL RELATIONS. Metuchen, N.J.: Scarecrow Press, 1967. xvii, 387 p.

A comprehensive listing of books published between 1955 and 1966 in the field of domestic and foreign politics. No annotations.

Universal Reference System. BIBLIOGRAPHY OF BIBLIOGRAPHIES IN POLITICAL SCIENCE, GOVERNMENT, AND PUBLIC POLICY. Political Science, Government, and Public Policy Series, vol. 3. Princeton, N.J.: Princeton Research Publishing Co., 1967. 927 p.

An exhaustive listing of bibliographical sources on government and politics with brief annotations. Because of its comprehensiveness, this volume will be most helpful for the advanced researcher.

_____. INTERNATIONAL AFFAIRS. Political Science, Government, and Public Policy Series, vol. 1. 2d ed. Princeton, N.J.: Princeton Research Publishing Co., 1969. xx, 1,206 p.

An annotated, indexed compilation of important books, pamphlets, and articles selected and processed by the Universal Reference System, a computerized information retrieval service. The volume is exhaustive and will be particularly useful to the specialized researcher. Annual supplements offered.

White, Carl M., and Associates. SOURCES OF INFORMATION IN THE SOCIAL SCIENCES. 2d ed. Chicago: American Library Association, 1973. 702 p.

An excellent introductory annotated guide to the social sciences. Nine different social science fields are examined (economics in chapter 4 and political science in chapter 9) and because of the quality of its annotations and organization, this volume is particularly valuable to the person exploring the literature in the various social sciences.

Zawodny, Janusz K. GUIDE TO THE STUDY OF INTERNATIONAL RELATIONS. San Francisco: Chandler Publishing Co., 1966. xii, 151 p.

An annotated guide to the most important information sources in international relations. The guide deals with bibliographies, dictionaries, guides, periodicals, and yearbooks.

Reference Materials

B. JOURNALS

AMERICAN ECONOMIC REVIEW
American Economic Association
1313 21st Avenue, South
Nashville, Tenn. 37212

1911--. Quarterly.

AMERICAN JOURNAL OF INTER-NATIONAL LAW
American Society of International Law
2223 Massachusetts Avenue, N.W.
Washington, D.C. 20008

1907--. Quarterly.

AMERICAN JOURNAL OF POLITICAL SCIENCE
Wayne State University Press
5980 Cass Avenue
Detroit, Mich. 48202

1957--. Quarterly.

AMERICAN POLITICAL SCIENCE REVIEW
American Political Science Association
1527 New Hampshire Avenue, N.W.
Washington, D.C. 20036

1906--. Quarterly.

THE ANNALS OF THE AMERICAN ACADEMY OF POLITICAL AND SOCIAL SCIENCE
American Academy of Political and Social Science
3937 Chestnut Street
Philadelphia, Pa. 19104

Bimonthly.

CHALLENGE
International Arts and Sciences Press
901 North Broadway
White Plains, N.Y. 10603

1952--. Bimonthly.

COLUMBIA JOURNAL OF TRANS-NATIONAL LAW
Columbia Journal of Transnational Law Association
Columbia University School of Law
New York, N.Y. 10027

1961--. Two-three issues per year.

CORNELL INTERNATIONAL LAW JOURNAL
Cornell University Law School
Myron Taylor Hall
Ithaca, N.Y. 14853

1968--. Two issues per year.

DAEDALUS
Journal of the American Academy of Arts and Sciences
Harvard University
7 Linden Street
Cambridge, Mass. 02138

1958--. Quarterly.

ECONOMIC DEVELOPMENT AND CULTURAL CHANGE
University of Chicago Press
5801 Ellis Avenue
Chicago, Ill. 60637

1952--. Quarterly.

FOREIGN AFFAIRS*
Council on Foreign Relations
58 East 68th Street
New York, N.Y. 10021

1922--. Quarterly.

FOREIGN POLICY*
National Affairs, in association with the Carnegie Endowment for International Peace
345 East 46th Street
New York, N.Y. 10017

1970--. Quarterly.

* Indicates journal of particular importance.

139

GOVERNMENT AND OPPOSITION:
A JOURNAL OF COMPARATIVE
POLITICS
Government and Opposition, with the
Assistance of the London School
of Economics and Political Science
Houghton Street
London WC2A 2AE, England

1965--. Quarterly.

HARVARD INTERNATIONAL LAW
JOURNAL
Harvard Law School
Cambridge, Mass. 02138

1959--. Three issues per year.

INTER-AMERICAN ECONOMIC
AFFAIRS*
Inter-American Affairs Press
P.O. Box 181
Washington, D.C. 20044

1947--. Quarterly.

INTERNATIONAL AFFAIRS*
Royal Institute of International Affairs
Oxford University Press
Press Road
Neasden, London N.W.10, England

1922--. Quarterly.

INTERNATIONAL ORGANIZATION*
Sponsored by the World Peace Founda-
tion
University of Wisconsin Press
Box 1379
Madison, Wis. 53701

1947--. Quarterly.

INTERNATIONAL STUDIES QUAR-
TERLY*
International Studies Association
Sage Publications
275 South Beverly Drive
Beverly Hills, Calif. 90212

1957--. Quarterly.

JOURNAL OF COMMON MARKET
STUDIES
Basil Blackwell
108 Cowley Road
Oxford OX4 1JF, England

1962--. Quarterly.

JOURNAL OF CONFLICT RESOLU-
TION
Sage Publications
275 South Beverly Drive
Beverly Hills, Calif. 90212

1957--. Quarterly.

JOURNAL OF DEVELOPING AREAS
Western Illinois University
Macomb, Ill. 61455

1966--. Quarterly.

JOURNAL OF DEVELOPMENT STUD-
IES
Frank Cass & Co.
67 Great Russell Street
London W.C.1, England

1964--. Quarterly.

JOURNAL OF INTERNATIONAL
AFFAIRS*
School of International Affairs
Columbia University
420 West 118th Street
New York, N.Y. 10027

1947--. Two issues per year.

JOURNAL OF INTERNATIONAL
ECONOMICS
North-Holland Publishing Co.
P.O. Box 211
Amsterdam, The Netherlands

1971--. Quarterly.

* Indicates journal of particular importance.

JOURNAL OF INTERNATIONAL LAW
AND ECONOMICS
National Law Center
George Washington University
Washington, D.C. 20052

    1966--. Three issues per year.

JOURNAL OF INTERNATIONAL LAW
AND POLITICS
New York University School of Law
40 Washington Square South
New York, N.Y. 10012

    Three issues per year.

JOURNAL OF PEACE RESEARCH
International Peace Research Institute
Universitetsforlaget, University of Oslo
Box 307
Blindern, Oslo 3, Norway

    1964--. Quarterly.

JOURNAL OF POLITICAL ECONOMY
University of Chicago Press
5801 Ellis Avenue
Chicago, Ill. 60637

    1892--. Bimonthly.

JOURNAL OF POLITICS
Southern Political Science Association
University of Florida
107 Peabody Hall
Gainesville, Fla. 32611

    1939--. Quarterly.

JOURNAL OF WORLD TRADE LAW
Vincent Press
60 Cole Park Road
Twickenham
Middlesex, England
    1967--. Bimonthly.

MILLENNIUM: JOURNAL OF INTER-
NATIONAL STUDIES
Millennium Publishing Group
Houghton Street
London WC2A 2AE, England

    1974--. Three issues per year.

ORBIS; A JOURNAL OF WORLD
AFFAIRS*
Foreign Policy Research Institute in
    association with the Fletcher
    School of Law and Diplomacy,
    Tufts University
3508 Market Street, Suite 350
Philadelphia, Pa. 19104

    1957--. Quarterly.

POLITICAL QUARTERLY
Political Quarterly Publishing Co.
49 Park Lane
London W.1, England

    1930--. Quarterly.

POLITICAL SCIENCE QUARTERLY
Academy of Political Science
Columbia University
413 Fayerweather Hall
New York, N.Y. 10027

    1886--. Quarterly.

POLITICAL STUDIES
Political Studies Association of the
    United Kingdom
Clarendon Press
Ely House
London W.1, England

    1953--. Quarterly.

SAIS REVIEW
School of Advanced International
    Studies
Johns Hopkins University
1740 Massachusetts Avenue, N.W.
Washington, D.C. 20036

    1956--. Quarterly.

* Indicates journal of particular importance.

SOCIAL RESEARCH
Graduate Faculty of Political and
    Social Science of the New School
    for Social Research
40 Sheridan Avenue
Albany, N.Y. 12210

    1934--. Quarterly.

WESTERN POLITICAL QUARTERLY
Western Political Science Association
Pacific Northwest Political Science
    Association
Southern California Political Science
    Association
University of Utah
Salt Lake City, Utah 84112

    1948--. Quarterly.

WORLD DEVELOPMENT
Pergamon Press
Headington Hill Hall
Oxford OX3 OBW, England

    1931--. Monthly.

WORLD POLITICS*
Center of International Studies
Princeton University
Princeton, N.J. 08540

    1948--. Quarterly.

WORLD TODAY
Royal Institute of International Affairs
Oxford University Press
Press Road
Neasden, London N.W.10, England

    1945--. Monthly.

* Indicates journal of particular importance.

Appendix
RECOMMENDED BOOKS

The books listed in this appendix are recommended for small libraries.

Adler-Karlsson, Gunner. WESTERN ECONOMIC WARFARE, 1947-1967; A CASE STUDY IN FOREIGN ECONOMIC POLICY. Stockholm: Humanities Press, 1968. 319 p.

Barnet, Richard J., and Mueller, Ronald E. GLOBAL REACH: THE POWER OF THE MULTINATIONAL CORPORATIONS. New York: Simon & Schuster, 1974. 478 p.

Bauer, Raymond A.; Pool, Ithiel de Sola; and Dexter, Lewis Anthony. AMERICAN BUSINESS AND PUBLIC POLICY; THE POLITICS OF FOREIGN TRADE. 2d ed. Chicago: Aldine-Atherton, 1972. 490 p.

Bergsten, C. Fred, and Krause, Lawrence B., eds. WORLD POLITICS AND INTERNATIONAL ECONOMICS. Washington, D.C.: Brookings Institution, 1975. xi, 359 p.

Boulding, Kenneth E., and Mukerjee, Tapan, eds. ECONOMIC IMPERIALISM: A BOOK OF READINGS. Ann Arbor: University of Michigan Press, 1972. xviii, 338 p.

Brown, Seyom. NEW FORCES IN WORLD POLITICS. Washington, D.C.: Brookings Institution, 1974. viii, 224 p.

Calleo, David P., and Rowland, Benjamin M. AMERICA AND THE WORLD POLITICAL ECONOMY: ATLANTIC DREAMS AND NATIONAL REALITIES. Bloomington: Indiana University Press, 1973. 360 p.

Clark, John J. THE NEW ECONOMICS OF NATIONAL DEFENSE. New York: Random House, 1966. 235 p.

Recommended Books

Cohen, Benjamin J. THE QUESTION OF IMPERIALISM: THE POLITICAL ECONOMY OF DOMINANCE AND DEPENDENCE. New York: Basic Books, 1973. 280 p.

Cox, Robert W., ed. THE POLITICS OF INTERNATIONAL ORGANIZATIONS. Papers prepared under the auspices of the International Political Science Association. New York: Praeger Publishers, 1970. 303 p.

Dougherty, James E., and Pfaltzgraff, Robert L., Jr. CONTENDING THEORIES OF INTERNATIONAL RELATIONS. New York: J.B. Lippincott Co., 1971. 416 p.

Doxey, Margaret P. ECONOMIC SANCTIONS AND INTERNATIONAL ENFORCEMENT. Published for the Royal Institute of International Affairs. London: Oxford University Press, 1971. 162 p.

Gilpin, Robert. U.S. POWER AND THE MULTINATIONAL CORPORATION: THE POLITICAL ECONOMY OF FOREIGN DIRECT INVESTMENT. New York: Basic Books, 1975. xii, 291 p.

Goldman, Marshall I. SOVIET FOREIGN AID. New York: Praeger Publishers, 1967. 258 p.

Holsti, K.J. INTERNATIONAL POLITICS: A FRAMEWORK FOR ANALYSIS. 2d ed. Englewood Cliffs, N.J.: Prentice-Hall, 1972. 532 p.

Johnson, Harry G. ECONOMIC POLICIES TOWARD LESS DEVELOPED COUNTRIES. New York: Praeger Publishers, 1968. 271 p.

Kenen, Peter B., and Lubitz, Raymond. INTERNATIONAL ECONOMICS. 3d ed. Englewood Cliffs, N.J.: Prentice-Hall, 1971. viii, 127 p.

Keohane, Robert O., and Nye, Joseph S., Jr. eds. TRANSNATIONAL RELATIONS AND WORLD POLITICS. Cambridge, Mass.: Harvard University Press, 1972. 398 p.

Kindleberger, Charles P. POWER AND MONEY; THE ECONOMICS OF INTERNATIONAL POLITICS AND THE POLITICS OF INTERNATIONAL ECONOMICS. New York: Basic Books, 1970. vi, 246 p.

Knorr, Klaus. THE POWER OF NATIONS; THE POLITICAL ECONOMY OF INTERNATIONAL RELATIONS. New York: Basic Books, 1975. x, 353 p.

Lichtheim, George. IMPERIALISM. New York: Praeger Publishers, 1971. 183 p.

Lindberg, Leon N., and Scheingold, Stuart A. EUROPE'S WOULD-BE POLITY: PATTERNS OF CHANGE IN THE EUROPEAN COMMUNITY. Englewood Cliffs, N.J.: Prentice-Hall, 1970. vi, 314 p.

Magdoff, Harry. THE AGE OF IMPERIALISM: THE ECONOMICS OF U.S. FOREIGN POLICY. New York: Monthly Review Press, 1969. 208 p.

Morgenthau, Hans. POLITICS AMONG NATIONS: THE STRUGGLE FOR POWER AND PEACE. 5th ed. New York: Alfred A. Knopf, 1973. 618 p.

O'Leary, Michael K. THE POLITICS OF AMERICAN FOREIGN AID. New York: Atherton Press, 1967. xiv, 172 p.

Packenham, Robert A. LIBERAL AMERICA AND THE THIRD WORLD. Princeton, N.J.: Princeton University Press, 1973. 378 p.

Pearson, Lester B., et al. PARTNERS IN DEVELOPMENT; REPORT OF THE COMMISSION OF INTERNATIONAL DEVELOPMENT. New York: Praeger Publishers, 1969. 395 p.

Rosen, Steven J., and Kurth, James R., eds. TESTING THEORIES OF ECONOMIC IMPERIALISM. Lexington, Mass.: Lexington Books, 1974. ix, 284 p.

Said, Abdul A., and Simmons, Luis R., eds. THE NEW SOVEREIGNS; MULTINATIONAL CORPORATIONS AS WORLD POWERS. Englewood Cliffs, N.J.: Prentice-Hall, 1975. vi, 186 p.

Vernon, Raymond. SOVEREIGNTY AT BAY: THE MULTINATIONAL SPREAD OF U.S. ENTERPRISES. New York: Basic Books, 1971. 326 p.

Wall, David. THE CHARITY OF NATIONS; THE POLITICAL ECONOMY OF AID. New York: Basic Books, 1973. 181 p.

Warnecke, Steven J., ed. THE EUROPEAN COMMUNITY IN THE 1970's. New York: Praeger Publishers, 1972. xviii, 228 p.

Wilber, Charles, ed. THE POLITICAL ECONOMY OF DEVELOPMENT AND UNDERDEVELOPMENT. New York: Random House, 1973. 434 p.

Wiles, P.J.D. COMMUNIST INTERNATIONAL ECONOMICS. New York: Praeger Publishers, 1968. 566 p.

Wolf, Charles, Jr. FOREIGN AID: THEORY AND PRACTICE IN SOUTHERN ASIA. Princeton, N.J.: Princeton University Press, 1960. 416 p.

AUTHOR INDEX

This index is alphabetized letter by letter and references are to page numbers. It includes authors, editors, translators, compilers, and contributors.

A

Abbott, C.C. 130
Ackermann, Frank 101, 110
Adams, Gordon 56
Adelman, M.A. 39, 91
Adler-Karlsson, Gunnar 42, 130, 143
Aitken, Thomas, Jr. 83
Ajami, Fuad 91, 96
Alba, Victor 29
Alexandrowicz, Charles H. 19
Alger, Chadwick F. 91
Aliber, Robert Z. 61
Alker, Hayward, Jr. 33
Allen, Robert L. 34, 130
Alnaswari, Abbas 29
Alpert, E.J. 68
Alting Von Geusau, Frans A.M. 34, 51, 62
Amin, Samir 101
Amir, Shimeon 78
Arnold, H.J.P. 78
Aron, Raymond 113
Asher, Robert E. 23, 67
Aubrey, Henry G. 19, 61
Avery, William P. 56
Azar, Edward E. 113

B

Bachmann, Hans 29

Backman, Jules 129
Baer, George W. 42
Baer, Werner 83
Bailey, Richard 51
Baird, Mary 74
Balassa, Bela 34, 47
Baldwin, David A. 20, 42, 72-73
Baldwin, H.W. 131
Baldwin, John 117
Baldwin, Robert E. 34
Baldwin, William L. 117
Banfield, Edward C. 73
Baran, Paul A. 4, 108
Barbera, Henry 113
Barkun, Michael 136
Barnet, Richard J. xxii, 91, 113, 143
Basch, Antonin 131
Baudin, Louis xxi, 113
Bauer, P.T. 39
Bauer, Raymond A. 34, 143
Beer, Francis A. 4
Behrman, Jack N. xx, 15, 83, 92
Benoit, Emile 117-18, 124
Bentil, J. Kodwo 56
Bergsten, C. Fred 4, 6, 15, 24, 39, 62, 143
Berliner, Joseph S. 78
Bernard, Stephen 118
Bernstein, Marvin 84
Bernstein, S.J. 68
Bhagwati, Jagdish N. 16, 19, 68

Author Index

Bidwell, Percy W. 24, 118-19, 129 131
Billerbeck, Klaus 78
Bird, Richard M. 73
Black, Eugene R. 68
Black, Lloyd A. 68
Blair, Patricia W. 20
Blanchard, Daniel S. 84
Blaug, Mark 101
Bleicher, Samuel A. 20
Bliss, Chester I. 9
Bloch, Henry S. 127
Boarman, Patrick M. 62
Bodenheimer, Susanne 108
Bolton, Roger E. 119
Boorman, James A. III 39
Bosman, Hans W.J. 62
Boulding, Kenneth E. 4, 102, 118, 119, 143
Bowley, Arthur L. 127
Brenner, Michael J. 51
Brester, Havelock 56
Breton, Albert 5
Broadbridge, Seymour 29
Brock, Clifton 135
Brodie, Bernard 114
Bronfenbrenner, Martin 84
Brown, E. Cary 121
Brown, Lester R. 73
Brown, Michael B. 108
Brown, Neville 114
Brown, Seyom 7, 143
Brown, William Adams, Jr. 73
Brown-John, C. Lloyd 42
Brundenius, Claes 108
Bryant, William E. 29
Bukharin, Nikolai I. 102
Burtis, David 135

C

Calleo, David P. 24, 143
Campbell, W. Glenn 127
Camps, Miriam 8, 51
Caporaso, James A. 47
Carnoy, Martin 57
Center for Strategic Studies. Georgetown University 119
Chadwick, Richard W. 8
Chandler, Geoffrey 92

Chandler, Lester V. 127
Chandrasekhar, Sripati 73
Cheever, Daniel S. 21
Chernotsky, Harry I. 109
Child, Sarah 29
Clark, John J. 127, 143
Clark, John M. 127
Clark, William H. 51
Claude, Inis L., Jr. 48
Clayton, James L. 128
Cleveland, Harlan 73
Cleveland, Harold van Buren 62
Clifford, J. 80
Cloan, John W. 56
Cobb, Stephen 119
Cochrane, James D. 56
Cohen, Benjamin J. xx, 25, 102, 144
Cohen, Stephen D. 62
Coleman, John R. 126
Condliffe, J.B. 120
Congress for Peace Through Law, Members of. See Members of Congress for Peace Through Law, Military Spending Committee
Coombes, David 51
Cooper, Richard N. 8, 16, 34, 62
Collick, Martin 29
Corbet, Hugh 16
Cordovez, Diego 20
Couloumbis, Theodore A. 97
Cox, Robert W. 18, 20, 21, 22, 63, 69, 144
Culbertson, W.S. 131
Curtin, Timothy R.C. 42
Curzon, Gerard 21, 51
Curzon, Victoria 51, 57
Cuthbert-Brown, John 31

D

Dahrendorf, Ralf 52
Dam, Kenneth W. 21, 40
Damm, Walter 97
Dangerfield, Roy 131
Davis, S. Sm. 84
Delaisi, Francis 42
Dell, Sidney 21, 57
Deutsch, Karl W. 8, 9, 102, 136
Dexter, Byron 136

Author Index

Author Index

TITLE INDEX

This index includes all titles of books and published reports which are cited in the text. In some cases titles have been shortened. Alphabetization is letter by letter.

Title Index

SUBJECT INDEX

This index is alphabetized letter by letter.   Underlined page numbers refer to main areas within the subject.

Subject Index

Latin American Free Trade Association
57, 58, 59, 60
Law. See International economic law
League of Nations 42, 43, 45
Lenin, Vladimir I. 102, 103, 109
Less developed countries xvi-xvii,
16, 102
capitalism in 70
cooperation among 18, 21
economic development of 3, 17
economic policies of 29
economic policies toward 7, 17,
24, 25, 28, 30, 51, 52, 54
foreign aid to 3, 17, 18, 24, 30,
67-81
foreign investment in 3, 16, 30,
71, 85, 86, 90, 91
foreign trade policies of 38, 39,
41, 109
interaction among 31-32
international organizations in 17,
18, 21, 22, 24
militarism in 69
multinational corporations in xviii,
xxii, 17, 91-92, 93, 95,
96, 97, 98, 100
planning in 17-18
regional integration in 56-60
as threats to peace 114
world integration and 19
Liberalism xx-xi, 113
Liquidity 61, 64
Loans, foreign
as foreign aid 72, 73
government promotion of 66
See also British Loan Agreements;
Investment, foreign
Lobbyists, influence on trade policy
34
Luxemburg, Rosa 102

M

Magdoff, Harry 105
Malawi, foreign aid to 69
Manufacturers 99. See also Industry
Marxist economic theories xix,
xxi-xxii, 17
on economic growth 4
on imperialism 101, 102, 103, 104,
105, 106, 107, 108, 109, 110

on the international monetary
system 64
on war 113, 114, 115
See also Socialism
Medicine, as foreign aid 77
Mercantilism xx-xxi, 17, 113. See
also Imperialism
Mexico, regional integration in 59
Migration, transnational 2
politics of 6, 11
See also Population
Militarism
imperialism and 105
in less developed countries 69
Military aid 70, 73, 74, 78
armed forces development and 69
relationship to economic assistance
28
relationship to military intervention
110-11
See also Foreign aid
Military expenditures. See Defense
Military occupation 127
Military research. See Research and
development
Mineral industries
foreign investment by 108
foreign policy and 10
See also names of specific mineral
industries
Money. See Dollar; Foreign exchange
rates; Gold; International
monetary system; Liquidity;
Pound sterling
Monopolies 40. See also Cartels
Moran, Theodore 105
Morocco, foreign investment in 88
Multinational corporations 2, 3
in the Common Market 52
foreign investments of xii, 17,
83-84, 87, 89, 91-100
imperialism and 107, 110
international economic phenomena
and xviii
politics of 6, 9, 10, 96
regulation of 92, 95, 99
See also Business; Joint ventures;
Mineral industries; Petroleum
industry
Multipolar international system xvi. See
also Bipolar international system